D0475756

*There is an art of reading
as well as an art of thinking
and an art of writing.*
ISAAC D'ISRAELI

The Art of
English

General Editor A. Dora Gough, B.A. (Hons.)

A Certificate Course for Secondary Schools

Keith Newson, M.A.

2

Illustrated by Tony Dyson

SCHOFIELD AND SIMS LIMITED
HUDDERSFIELD

0 7217 0004 7

First Printed 1965
Reprinted 1966
Reprinted 1968
Reprinted 1969
Reprinted 1970
Reprinted 1971
Revised and Reprinted 1971
Reprinted 1973
Reprinted 1974
Reprinted 1975
Reprinted (twice) 1976
Revised and Reprinted 1977

Printed by Letts Erskine Ltd., Dalkeith
Bound in Scotland

Contents

Each chapter contains a passage and the following sections:

> For Discussion
> For Written Answers
> Method Exercises
> Writing Your Own
> Things To Do
> Books To Read

Some chapters include a poem and a section "Discussing the Poem".

The following Contents List includes the new work (but not the further practice) introduced in the Method Exercises in each chapter.

ACKNOWLEDGMENTS

The author and publishers wish to thank the following for permission to include the copyright material listed below:

Putnam & Co. Ltd., (and the New Windmill Series, William Heinemann Ltd.) for an extract from *The Otterbury Incident* by C. Day Lewis.

For the poem *Child on Top of a Greenhouse* from *The Lost Son and Other Poems*. New York: Doubleday & Company, 1948; London: J. Lehmann, 1949. Copyright Beatrice Roethke as administratrix of the estate of Theodore Roethke.
Also: *Child on Top of a Greenhouse* copyright 1946 by Editorial Publications, Inc., from *Words for the Wind* by Theodore Roethke. Reprinted by permission of Doubleday & Company, Inc.

J. M. Dent & Sons Ltd., for an extract from *Clarion Call* by James Stagg, and an extract from *She Shall Have Music* by Kitty Barne.

Oxford University Press for an extract from *Tom's Midnight Garden* by A. Philippa Pearce.

The Literary Trustees of Walter de la Mare and the Society of Authors as their representative for the poems *The Listeners* and *Snow*.

Wm. Collins, Sons & Co. Ltd., for an extract from *The Secret Dog* by Diana Pullein-Thompson.

MacGibbon & Kee Ltd., for an extract from *Greeks and Trojans* by Rex Warner.

Methuen & Co. Ltd., for an extract from *Castaway Christmas* by Margaret J. Baker and the poem *Smells* from *Chimney Smoke* by Christopher Morley.

Pickering & Inglis Ltd., and Holt, Rinehart and Winston, Inc., New York, for an extract from *Mayflower Boy* by Stanley Young, Copyright 1944 by Stanley Young. Reprinted by permission of Holt, Rinehart and Winston, Inc., Publishers, New York.

John Murray (Publishers) Ltd., for an extract from *Scott's Last Expedition* (From the Personal Journals of Capt. R. F. Scott, CVO, R.N.).

A. & C. Black Ltd., for an extract from *Carcajou* by Rutherford Montgomery.

George G. Harrap & Co. Ltd., for an extract from *The Haircut* from *The Goalkeeper's Revenge and Other Stories* by Bill Naughton.

Thomas Nelson & Sons Ltd., for an extract from *The Swish of the Curtain* by Pamela Brown.

Mrs. E. F. Starkey for the poem *Nelson Street* by Seumas O'Sullivan.

William Heinemann Ltd., for an extract from *The Saturdays* by Elizabeth Enright, and an extract from *The Maythorn Story* by Geoffrey Trease.

Holt, Rinehart and Winston, Inc., New York, for an extract from *The Saturdays* by Elizabeth Enright. Copyright 1941 by Elizabeth Enright Gillham. Reprinted by permission of Holt, Rinehart and Winston, Inc., Publishers, New York.

Eyre & Spottiswoode (Publishers) Ltd., for an extract from *My Friend Flicka* by Mary O'Hara.

For the poem *The Runaway* by Robert Frost from *The Complete Poems of Robert Frost*, Publishers Jonathan Cape Limited, Proprietors, Holt, Rinehart and Winston, Inc.
Also: From *The Complete Poems of Robert Frost*. Copyright 1923 by Holt, Rinehart and Winston, Inc. Copyright renewed 1951 by Robert Frost. Reprinted by permission of Holt, Rinehart and Winston, Inc., New York.

Jonathan Cape Limited, for an extract from *The Silver Sword* by Ian Serraillier, and an extract from *Wintercut* by Elizabeth Grove.

Miss J. Freeman for the poem *Music Comes* by John Freeman from *Fresh Fields* (school poetry anthology) ed. E. W. Parker, published by Longmans Green & Company Limited.

For the poem *Caliban in the Coal Mines* by Louis Untermeyer. Copyright, 1914, by Harcourt Brace & World, Inc.; renewed, 1942, by Louis Untermeyer and reprinted from his volume, *Long Feud*, by permission of the publishers.

Rupert Hart-Davis Ltd., for an extract from *The Fair to Middling* by Arthur Calder Marshall.

Hutchinson & Co. (Publishers) Ltd., for an extract from *Along the Edge of the Sea* by Jill Norman.

W. W. E. Ross, Esq., for his poem *The Diver* from *The Penguin Book of Canadian Verse*.

The owners of the copyright of the following poems are not known. While efforts to discover these continue we venture to include:
The Fog by F. R. McCreary. *The David Jazz* by Edwin Meade Robinson.

Telegram Form p. 96 by courtesy of H. M. Postmaster General.

New Ministry of Transport Signs pp. 19, 20 by permission.

AUTHOR'S NOTE

THE ART OF ENGLISH is a five year English series for secondary schools, comprising two complete but closely integrated courses. The *Certificate Course* is suitable for those pupils in grammar, comprehensive and modern schools who aim at an Ordinary Level Certificate in English Language. The *General Course* is designed for the less academic pupils in comprehensive and modern schools. The two courses are planned on a common basis, and the obvious similarities in topics and layout can be readily appreciated by pupil as well as teacher. Transfer from one course to another is greatly facilitated, and both courses cover work for the Certificate of Secondary Education, though the approaches naturally differ.

The *Certificate Course* was devised in the belief that examination success should be the natural outcome of a wide and stimulating range of experience, and it is hoped that this course will be more than an English language textbook. The choice of verse and prose extracts is intended to develop pupils' reading, to sharpen their critical awareness of literature as an aspect of the real world around them, to inspire their interests in acting, in discussion of contemporary problems, and in finding out for themselves, and particularly to prompt and guide their natural wish to express themselves fluently and well.

Together, The *Certificate* and The *General Courses* form the basis for a complete English syllabus for secondary schools.

Book Two of The *Certificate Course* continues to base the work on substantial extracts taken from good, modern books that pupils are then encouraged to read for themselves; but each extract has its own interest and appeal, and is used as a basis for class discussion, to prompt further reading and simple research, and above all as a stimulus to written work. The whole range of composition is included, and personal and free verse writing are particularly encouraged. In the grammar work, which the course will develop to meet the most rigorous demands of the Ordinary Level Certificate Examination, the emphasis on creative and constructive exercises which will lead to an understanding of English usage has been maintained. The conventional "graphic analysis" approach is covered in the Supplementary Exercises for those who wish to augment the work in this way. Other revision exercises are also included.

In addition to acknowledging generous help from Wandsworth Borough Libraries and particularly from Mrs Doris Aubrey, I should like to thank Mrs Isobel Evans and other members of the Hertfordshire Library Service for help with recommendations for "Books to Read".   KEITH NEWSON

Ted and Toppy, on the trail of a vicious crook called Johnny Sharp and his assistant, the Wart, have ventured into the cellar of Skinner's warehouse where they have discovered cases of stolen cigarettes and a coiner's den. Suddenly they hear the crooks returning.

CHAPTER ONE

Trespassing

"The trap-door. Quick!" said Toppy.

They tore up the chute. But, as they reached the top, they saw the big warehouse door beginning to open. Toppy, who was ahead, managed to scramble through the trap; he flitted like a bat towards the staircase that led up to the workshop. In the mad *sauve-qui-peut*, his foot had accidentally thrust against Ted, who slid a little way down the chute. By the time he had scrambled up to the trap-door again, the Wart and Johnny Sharp, their backs turned to him, were in the warehouse, only six yards away. Frantically, Ted tugged at the trap-door. It would be fatal if the men found it open. It slid back silently over his head. This was a respite at any rate. He careered down the chute, through the vault, into the passage beyond, bumping and bruising himself against the edge of a packing-case, for the sliding to of the trap had automatically switched off the electric lights in the vault. He paused a moment by the door of the coiner's den. There seemed to be no sounds of pursuit. Perhaps the roar of the lorry's engine had covered up the noise he made on the chute. He remembered he'd brought a pocket-torch. Switching it on, he turned off the light in the den, closed the splintered door, and crept off along the passage away from the vaults.

The passage took him about twenty paces. Then there was a flight of stone steps. Climbing up these, he found a blank wall, a grating set high up in it, and a small door. Desperately he tugged at its handle. The door was locked.

Ted knew it was only a matter of minutes before the gang realised something was wrong. The dressing-table moved out of

9

position in the warehouse; the packing-case Toppy had opened; the splintered door of the coiner's den—there were too many signs betraying him. He sat down on the stone steps, his head in his hands, trying to steady his nerve. There was only one hope—that the gang would go upstairs first, find the scout-rope dangling from the workshop skylight, and assume that their birds had flown. But would Toppy have the sense to leave the rope there? Wouldn't his instinct be to remove this indication of their presence?

Then Ted caught at another straw of hope. Up above, in a cubby-hole off the workshop, there was a telephone. Perhaps Toppy had had time and sense enough to ring up the police before making his escape. If the gang found him, Ted determined that he would play this card, even though it might only be a bluff.

Even as he made this decision, he heard footsteps approaching along the passage, and a voice—the soft, cold voice of Johnny Sharp—saying, "Come out! Come on out! And no tricks."

(from The Otterbury Incident by C. Day Lewis)

For Discussion

1. How, as far as you can tell from the passage, had the boys reached the coiner's den (from their first entry into the warehouse)?
2. What do you think had been the dressing-table's position, before they moved it?
3. What was above the warehouse?
4. Where did the gang find Ted?
5. What kind of persons do you imagine (a) Ted and (b) Johnny Sharp to be?
6. What do these expressions mean?

   their birds had flown   play this card
   straw of hope   a bluff
7. "Sauve-qui-peut" means "flight in which every man looks to his own safety". Why did the author use this French phrase here, instead of some English equivalent?
8. Explain: "Wouldn't his instinct be to remove this indication of their presence?" What does "instinct" mean here?
9. What damage had the boys done?
10. What is wrong about trespassing? Is it ever legal? Give instances where you think it would be justified.

For Written Answers

1. Write out the three or four words that tell us how Toppy ran from the trap-door to the staircase.
2. Write down (a) the adverb that tells us that Toppy did not mean to push Ted back down the chute, and (b) the adverb that shows us that the lights in the vault were beyond Ted's control.
3. Write down the other word used in the passage instead of "cellar".
4. Why was Ted in the dark?
5. What do you think Ted and Toppy heard to warn them of the crooks' return?

   (Answer questions 4 and 5 fully, in complete statement sentences.)

11

Child on Top of a Greenhouse

The wind billowing out the seat of my britches,
My feet crackling splinters of glass and dried putty,
The half-grown chrysanthemums staring up like accusers,
Up through the streaked glass, flashing with sunlight,
A few white clouds all rushing eastward,
A line of elms plunging and tossing like horses,
And everyone, everyone pointing up and shouting!

THEODORE ROETHKE

Discussing The Poem

1. Whom is this poem supposed to be spoken by? What has happened to him and how does the poem emphasize his feelings?
2. What kind of day is it? How does the poem emphasize this?
3. Can you describe a similar experience?

Method Exercises

The following extracts from the passage include four statements, one incomplete statement, two questions, one command, one incomplete command and one exclamation.
Discuss which are which:
> "The trap-door. Quick!"
> They tore up the chute.
> Frantically, Ted tugged at the trap-door.
> It slid back silently over his head.
> But would Toppy have the sense to leave the rope there?
> Wouldn't his instinct be to remove this indication of their presence?
> Perhaps Toppy had had time and sense enough to ring up the police before making his escape.
> "Come on out! And no tricks."

What is missing in the case of the incomplete statement and command?

Exercise 1. The following are incomplete or condensed sentences that might be used as newspaper or advertisement headlines. Rewrite them as full sentences, to give the full meanings.
> e.g., Election Soon.
> means: There will soon be an election.
> or: An election will soon take place.

Those marked with an asterisk* could have two meanings.

(a) No Hope for Mine Victims.
(b) Best Car Bargains Here.
(c) Couple Married Twice.
(d) Arsenal Won, Chelsea Too.
(e) Arsenal One, Chelsea Two.
(f) *Meat Talks in Whitehall.
(g) Best Buys at Bottomley's.
(h) Council Running Lottery.
(i) Price's Prices Down.
(j) *Student Riots in Oxford.

Nouns are names of persons, places, things or ideas. Those that name particular persons, places or things are called proper nouns. How can we recognize the proper nouns in the following sentence?

> Mr. Smith went to the smith who worked in the forge in Forge Lane.

Can you find twenty-one instances of the capital letter used for a proper noun in the introductory note and the passage from *The Otterbury Incident?*

Exercise 2. Rewrite the following, putting in all the capital letters, full stops, question marks and exclamation marks (50 in all) that are necessary.

> "did you have a good holiday, bill" asked his friend, george, when they met for the first time that term
>
> "you bet" bill replied his eyes lit up with enthusiasm "sam and i went to france, to paris, with the school party we climbed the eiffel tower, saw the mona lisa, were nearly run over at the arc de triomphe, went round notre dame, were photographed in montmartre, took a coach out to versailles for the day and went on a cruise up the river seine i reckon we saw just about everything"
>
> "you didn't go to the folies bergeres" george said doubtfully
>
> "no, but mr pearce and mr jenkins took some of the sixth formers out late on friday, and roberts says he saw one of them with a programme from there on saturday morning"
>
> "huh that proves nothing," commented george

Exercise 3. We saw in Book One that the same word can very often be either a noun or an adjective, according to how it is used. State whether the words in italics in the following sentences are nouns or adjectives. If the word is a noun, compose a sentence using it as an adjective; if it is an adjective, compose a sentence using it as a noun.

> e.g., He was a well-known television personality.
> Here "television" is an adjective.
> As a noun: Television has brought great changes in our way of life.

(a) We travelled on a *London* bus.
(b) The *proud* are easily discomforted.
(c) Let the cobbler stick to his *last*.
(d) The *student* teachers were all present.
(e) The *roof* beams were rotten.
(f) We employed a *house* painter.
(g) The *barn* owl watched us.
(h) We left the *stable* open.
(i) The *bicycle* was left by the wall.
(j) The *Dutch* find *English* easy to learn.

Exercise 4. (a) Many words do have special noun, adjective and adverb endings. (What is the difference between an adjective and an adverb?) In each of the following, the three sentences require the noun, adjective and adverb forms respectively. For each, write down the two that have been omitted;

> e.g., It was an *accident*.   (Noun)
> It was an *accidental* mistake. (Adjective)
> It happened *accidentally*.   (Adverb)

  i. The song was a thing of great *beauty*.
    It was a —— song.
    She sang it ——.

 ii. The *danger* was obvious.
    There was a —— corner ahead.
    The driver approached it ——.

iii. Dad was in a —— to go out.
    He ate a *hurried* tea.
    He ate it ——.

 iv. She was giving me her full *attention*.
    She was ——.
    She listened ——.

  v. He ran a ——.
    He was a very *busy* man.
    He worked ——.

 vi. The child was in ——.
    His was —— behaviour.
    He had behaved *disgracefully*.

vii. The hero showed great ——.
    He was *modest*.
    He —— praised his fellow soldiers.

viii. The carpenter's —— comes from practice.
    A —— carpenter knows how to use a chisel.
    He uses it *skilfully*.

ix. —— was the keynote of their design.
The *simple* design was the best one.
The boys designed it ——.

x. I was full of —— for their work.
Their work was ——.
They had done it *admirably*.

(b) Although many adverbs are formed by adding -ly to an adjective, many words ending in -ly are *not* adverbs. Rearrange the following words in three columns, one of words that are *normally* adjectives, one of adverbs, and one of nouns.

bully, chilly, family, filly, fully, friendly, galley, ghostly, grimly, poorly, pulley, purely, saucily, silly, unsightly.

Exercise 5. A vocabulary and spelling test: in the following, the number of dashes indicates the number of letters in the word that fits the definition, and the first letter or letters have been given to you.

e.g., The third day of the week (prop. n.): Tuesday

(a) The country of the Belgians (prop. n.): B - - - - - -
(b) Of unknown authorship (adj.): an - - - - - - -
(c) In a certain way, with certainty (adv.): de - - - - - - - -
(d) In an awkward or clumsy way (adv.): c - - - - - - -
(e) Opposite of guilty (adj.): in - - - - - -
(f) Full of knowledge, well-informed (adj.): k - - - - - - - - - - -
(g) In so obvious a way as to be noticed (adv.): no - - - - - - - -
(h) An inhabitant of Norway (prop. n.): N - - - - - - - -
(i) In a stealthy or cautious manner (adv.): st - - - - - - - -
(j) The fourth day of the week (prop. n.): W - - - - - - - -
(k) Any means of land transport on wheels (n.): v - - - - - -
(l) Full of virtue (adj.): v - - - - - - -
(m) Male equivalent of spinster (masc. n.): b - - - - - - -
(n) In a way that can be heard (adv.): au - - - - -

Writing Your Own

Most people have trespassed on private property at some time, either by accident or on purpose: perhaps when fishing, or when retrieving a lost ball. Most of us know the tense, slightly guilty feelings we have if we think we hear the owner or anyone in authority approaching. Can you remember clearly some occasion when *you* were trespassing, defying rules, or doing something wrong? Try to relive in your mind the nervous tension (perhaps the way every slight sound would make you jump), and describe the experience as vividly as you can in your own words. If you can honestly say you have never had such an experience, then try to imagine what it would be like.

Choose your words carefully: use adverbs (words like "frantically, silently, desperately" are effectively used in the passage), as well as adjectives, nouns and lively verbs ("tore, flitted, scrambled, careered" give the passage a great sense of excitement). Use some comparisons also, such as "like a bat" in the passage, and "chrysanthemums . . . like accusers" and "plunging and tossing like horses" in the poem.

Choose a title to suit your own composition, such as:

"THE DAY I WAS CAUGHT TRESPASSING"

18

Things To Do

1. Find out what you can about the law of trespass and other laws that affect our ordinary daily lives.

Can you be prosecuted just for being on private land? What is a right of way? If you see a path marked on an ordnance survey map, can you claim the right to follow that route?

What happens if a person your age is charged by the police?

What is the difference between a judge, a stipendiary magistrate and an ordinary magistrate, or J.P.? What is meant by "the bench", a juvenile court, a probation officer, petty sessions and quarter sessions?

Are cyclists allowed on *all* main roads, even if there is a special cycle track? Does a cyclist have to observe traffic signals when he is wheeling his cycle? Is a cyclist allowed (a) to park his cycle where there are "no waiting" restrictions, (b) to carry a passenger and (c) to ride without brakes? How are parking meters used? What is a ticket fine? Can a dog owner *ever* allow his dog off a lead on a road where dogs have to be kept on a lead?

What is the difference between square, round and triangular shaped traffic signs?

white on blue

black on white
with red border

white on blue

What do the following signs mean?

1
red circle and
cross on blue

2

3

white on blue

4

black on white
with red bar & circle

5

6

black on white with red borders

2. Work out a mime, or an impromptu play, of the incident in
the passage, or of that in the poem. In either case you will
probably want to extend and elaborate the story. Different
members of the class take particular parts and try to work out
the character and mannerisms of that person. Then the incident
has to be rehearsed, with each character working out his movements, timing and dialogue to fit in with the others. No script
should be necessary if actors are prepared to rehearse and work
out the action together.

3. Write a free verse poem about a dramatic or frightening
experience like that of the child on top of the greenhouse. Make
notes and work on them until you are left with a very "stream-
lined" version of the story, with just the vivid central ideas
emphasized, as in the poem by Roethke.

Books To Read

The Otterbury Incident by C. DAY LEWIS (Bodley Head; Heinemann; Penguin)
Most of the adventures of Ted, Toppy and their followers are narrated by one of the boys. These adventures really started when a school window was broken by a football and the boys clubbed together to raise the money to replace it.

The Pit by REGINALD MADDOCK (Collins; Macmillan)
A young boy struggles to prove his innocence when he is accused of stealing funds from the school shop. Butch's reactions to the local prejudice against him are portrayed with perception and sympathy.

A Wicked Pack of Cards by ROSEMARY HARRIS (Faber)
This gripping thriller revolves round the death of an old fortune-teller, the capacity of 9-year-old Culbertson Halliford to spy out the truth, and the problems 25-year-old Aunt Jane has in deciding whom to marry.

The Mystery of the Cross-Eyed Man by PAUL BERNA (translated by J. Buchanon-Brown) (Bodley Head; Penguin)
A fast-moving detective story by the author of "A Hundred Million Francs", in which Daniel and his younger brother find themselves stranded in Paris and forced to hitch-hike without money across France, followed by a sinister, cross-eyed stranger.

The Law by MICHAEL GILBERT (David and Charles)
The author sets out to explain what a solicitor's life is like and how this branch of the law works. He is a solicitor and a thriller writer himself, and makes this complicated subject readable and personal. (Classified as 340.023)

Young Charles Heston is confined to a wheel-chair, but he is well qualified to become editor of the weekly local newspaper that his friends, the Weighs, decide to bring out in support of their family campaign to save a local beauty spot, the Brimmacombe Heronry.

CHAPTER TWO

Magazine

Ruth and Rob soon proved that inexperience is no drawback in the collection of news. Ruth altered her hair style to make herself look more mature, as she put it. She drew it straight back off her forehead to form a sort of vertical roll behind, and it was most attractive. Rob grinned and suggested that he should wear a false beard to make him look older than his fifteen years. They operated together at first to give each other confidence, but were soon working separately, dividing the routine police, fire and hospital calls which they made every morning before school.

They wrote up their stories in the evenings—an additional chore to their homework—and put them in the wire tray on the table in the living room, which was my office. I then edited them and Sara, who was taking typing lessons, typed them on to a trial foolscap sheet.

We had started work on the Monday in order to have a full week in which to produce the paper, so that on Saturday we would all be free to distribute the *Clarion*. In this Harold Bourne again proved a most useful ally. He undertook to put a copy of the *Clarion* with each of the newspapers his three paper boys delivered, in addition to keeping a supply in the shop and handing one to each customer.

Sam took photographs of the Heronry and some of the views from it and developed them himself. By Wednesday all the features—Mr. Weigh's crusading piece called "Save the Heronry!", Helen's woman's page, and Harold Bourne's historical feature—were complete. All we had to do then, were the news pages and those would be left until last thing Thursday, so that we could go to press with the latest news possible.

On Friday morning Mrs. Weigh took our prototype copy of the first issue of the *Clarion* to Harold Bourne, and helped him to make hundreds of reproductions of each of the four sheets—both sides.

In the evening Sara, Pete and I pinned the four sheets together hundreds and hundreds of times, with one of those patent staplers. Pete had been taken off reporting—at his own request. He found his spelling a complete liability, amongst other drawbacks. Pete was what is called a late developer. As Daphne Weigh used to say of Pete: "He's got all his marbles, bless him, but he won't bring them out to play with yet. I'll just bet Pete will turn out the real genius of the family."

He was quite happy to be copy boy on the *Clarion*, and he ran to and fro between patient, sweet Sara—who slowly and lovingly typed away, with the tip of her tongue between her teeth—and me at my editorial desk.

Mrs. Weigh may have given me the title of Editor, but it was Rob, with his quick mind and terrific enthusiasm, with his surprising knowledge of how a newspaper is run, who was the real power. With his pleasantly ugly face set in thought and concentration, a thick strand of his fair hair falling over his forehead, he came to my rescue when I was struggling to get the pages laid out, so that we could cram as much as possible in them without them looking like a solid mass of type. In the end Rob and I had a weekly conference each Wednesday, when he would plan how the stories and features should be laid out.

Dear old Rob! He always "suggested" we do this or that. Or: "What do you say, Boy—shall we do it this way? You're the boss." But I knew better.

Mrs. Weigh was our artist, printing all our headlines and drawing our masthead each week, in addition to taking our copy to the "printers".

Sam's job as photographer suited him down to the ground. Sam was the most restless of the Weighs, and the constant movement entailed in looking for pictures to take, satisfied his lively spirit.

And so the first issue of the *Clarion* came out on time.

(from *Clarion Call* by James Stagg)

For Discussion

1. Why did Ruth and Rob operate together at first and separately later?
2. Why did they make the "routine calls" mentioned?
3. Why was Sam glad to be photographer?
4. What do you think "editing" involved?
5. Why was Pete not a success as a reporter? What qualities does a good reporter need?
6. Why was Sara's typing "slow and loving"?
7. How can a face be "pleasantly ugly"?
8. What qualities in Rob made him particularly suitable for newspaper work? How might experience have helped him even more?
9. How many pages did the *Clarion* have? How were they fixed together? How are newspapers and magazines normally fixed?
10. What are the advantages and disadvantages of producing an amateur newspaper or magazine as often as once a week?
11. Daphne Weigh was an American (she had married an Englishman): is there anything typically American about her speech?
12. How is it indicated in this passage that "Boy" was Charles's nickname? Why are "suggested" and "printers" in inverted commas?
13. What do the following mean?

stories	go to press	reproductions	masthead
features	prototype copy	copy boy	

For Written Answers

1. Work out the jobs done by various members of the production team of the *Clarion* in a table starting thus:

    Charles Heston . . . . Editor

    Mrs. Daphne Weigh . . . . . .

2. Describe in your own words the time-table for producing the *Clarion* each week.
3. What, if anything, did they charge for copies of the *Clarion*? How were they distributed?
4. What kind of shop did Mr. Harold Bourne own?
5. Why were the stories typed on to a "trial foolscap sheet"?

Method Exercises

Exercise 1. (a) You will remember from Book One that *verbs* are used in different *tenses*, to indicate whether the action took place in the past, or is taking place in the present, or will take place in the future. Thus the verb frequently consists of two or more words, not necessarily written next to each other:

   The "Clarion" *came* out on time. (Past)

   The "Clarion" *is coming* out on time. (Present)

(N.B. "The 'Clarion' *has come* out on time" is also present tense.)

   Will the "Clarion" *be coming* out on time? (Future)

In the following sentences, adapted from the passage, the fifteen verbs are printed in italics. Write out each verb and state its tense.

   i. Ruth and Rob soon *proved* that inexperience *is* no drawback.
   ii. Ruth *altered* her hair to make herself look more mature, as she *put* it.
   iii. We *had started* work on the Monday.
   iv. Pete *was* what *is called* a late developer.
   v. He *has got* all his marbles, but he *will* not *bring* them out.
   vi. Pete *will turn out* the real genius.
   vii. "What *do* you *say*, Boy—*shall* we *do* it this way? You *are* the boss." But I *knew* better.
   viii. Mrs. Weigh *was* our artist.

(b) Each of the verbs in the sentences in (a) has a *subject*—a noun or pronoun which limits it in *person* (first, second or third) and *number* (singular or plural). Thus the subjects of the verb *proved* in (a) i. are:

Ruth and Rob—3rd person, plural.

The subject of the verb *is* in (a) i. is:

inexperience—3rd person, singular.

And the subject of the verb *put* in (a) ii. is:

she—3rd person singular.

Give the subjects of the remaining twelve verbs (in numbers ii. to viii.), in a similar form.

Exercise 2. In the sentences used in Exercise 1, several of the verbs consisted of more than one word—these we can call VERB CLUSTERS:

had started   is called   will . . . bring

In each case one word (or part of a word) alone indicates what verb we are using:

had *start*ed   is *call*ed   will . . . *bring*.

"Start", "call" and "bring" can be called ROOT VERBS or HEAD-WORDS. Study the following verbs or verb clusters, where the head-words are in italics:

Birds *fly*.
Birds have *flown*.
Birds will be *fly*ing.
Birds may have been *fly*ing.
Birds will go on *fly*ing.
Birds ought to *fly*.

Write out the complete verb clusters in the following sentences, and then underline the head-word of the verb.

e.g. He was always eating sweets.

Answer: was . . . <u>eating</u>.

(Note that "always" is an adverb—saying *when* he was eating—and not part of the verb.)

(a) He has been eating all day.
(b) We shall be eating soon.
(c) I still have to do my homework.
(d) She has already done hers.
(e) Mother had cooked some more mince pies.
(f) The mince pies ought to be cooked by now.
(g) The sweep did not mince his words.
(h) He was going to sweep the chimney.
(i) Sweep the room, please.
(j) Will you be sweeping for long?

Exercise 3. In the following nine sentences we have used made-up subjects and verbs. Can you again recognise and write out the verb clusters and underline the head-words?

e.g. A dib was solemnly bangling.

Answer: was . . . <u>bangling</u>.

(a) Dibs bangle.
(b) Dibs have bangled.
(c) Dibs will be bangling.
(d) Dibs may have been bangling.
(e) Bangle all dibs.
(f) Have you been bangling the dibs?
(g) Can you dib a bangle?
(h) He certainly dibs bangles.
(i) Dibs might still be bangling, or bangles might want to dib.

Exercise 4. One of the difficulties in English spelling comes in words that contain SILENT LETTERS—letters which are no longer pronounced, nor used to alter the pronunciation of any other letters in the word. These are usually letters that *were* pronounced several hundred years ago, and in a few cases they are still pronounced in some dialects of English; for instance, in Scotland the -gh- in "night" is sometimes still pronounced as a -ch- sound.

Although silent letters have no function in spoken English, they do sometimes help differentiate between words of similar sound but different meaning, as in:

knot—not	knight—night
wring—ring	buoy—boy
reign—rain	sought—sort

Write down as many of the following words as you can, with correct spelling, using your dictionary to check the others.

e.g. Song of praise (to God), n. hymn

(a) A sacred song (in the Old Testament), n. p____
(b) Line (of persons, etc.) waiting their turn, n. q____
(c) Metre or beat of verse or music, n. r____   ·
(d) Struggle with or against, grapple, v. w____
(e) Crease in the skin (produced by age, etc.), n. w____
(f) Cover, for persons or parcels, n. w____
(g) Dweller next door or nearby, n. n____
(h) Draw a deep breath (expressing sadness, etc.), v. s____
(i) Faculty of vision; thing seen, n. s____
(j) Goblin or dwarf, n. g____
(k) Bite persistently, v. g____
(l) Work up into a dough or paste, v. k____
(m) Cutting instrument with two blades pivoted, n.pl. s____
(n) Place where something occurs, part of a play, n. s____
(o) Light sailing vessel for racing, n. y____
(p) Yellow part of an egg, n. y____
(q) Promoting health; good, a. w____
(r) Person entertained at one's house, n. g____
(s) Sentry; official in charge of a train, etc., n. g____
(t) Shelved closet or cabinet, n. c____

29

Exercise 5. In Book One we considered *abstract nouns*: the names of qualities, feelings, states, such as courage, anxiety, efficiency, generosity. Many of these nouns have corresponding adjectives: anger—angry, honesty—honest, patience—patient. (a) In the following, substitute its corresponding adjective for each abstract noun, as in this example:

Sara's patience—*patient* Sara.

i. a rival's envy
ii. Sam's restlessness
iii. the grass's smoothness
iv. a night's discomfort
v. the young prince's hope

vi. a miser's meanness
vii. old men's miserliness
viii. a shopkeeper's annoyance
ix. the boy's misery
x. the villain's cowardice.

(b) In the remaining ten, you have to make up the phrase using the abstract noun. This will mean using an *apostrophe* to show possession, since the quality belongs to some person(s) or thing(s). To revise the correct use of the apostrophe, turn to page 67.

e.g. those strong girders—those girders' *strength*.

i. a long liner
ii. its wide decks
iii. this lively photographer
iv. three rude children
v. a proud tigress

vi. a lovely princess
vii. her humble suitors
viii. this punctual patient
ix. the impatient fans
x. the two confident reporters.

Writing Your Own

Start work on some article or other contribution for a class magazine. If it is an informative article, about a hobby, a game or something that interests you, you will need to spend time in a library first, collecting information. At this stage, make rough notes, and remember to write down the title, author and page numbers (or chapter) of each book from which you take information, so that you can quickly refer back to check any details. Also, make rough sketches of any maps, drawings or diagrams you are going to include. The next stage will be to write up the complete article in full, with careful attention to spelling, to writing in sentences, and to dividing the article into paragraphs.

If you are going to interview someone or collect information or views from people, your first task will be to work out in detail the questions you want to ask, or the kind of information you are seeking.

If you are working on a crossword, a quiz or other puzzle, or a comic article, you will have to spend some time making sure that you have all your questions or information right, and arranged in the most effective way.

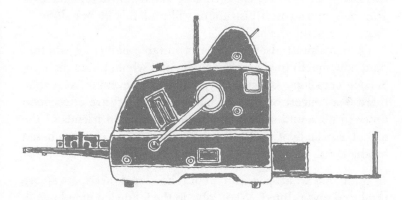

Things To Do

1. See if the class can be organized to produce their own form magazine or newspaper. Producing one issue a week, as Charles Heston and the Weighs did, may involve too much time and effort, but at least the class can aim at one complete number to be produced during the term.

How you reproduce your magazine will depend on the facilities available. Probably your school will have a duplicator, and if it and the paper are available, you can print pages and staple them together, as the Weighs did. Find out what the machine will do, whether it can reproduce illustrations or photographs at all, and whether you have to type articles on special stencils or with special carbons. If no form of duplicator is available, then at least the magazine could be typed or written out with carbon copies, say four or five copies in all, to be passed round the class and their friends, or alternatively the whole magazine can be neatly written out (on single sides) and pinned up on the notice-board.

To organize the magazine, it is a good idea to elect an editorial committee to select and arrange the material for each number. One committee member can be editor and write the Editorial. Other members of the class will be feature-writers, leader-writers, reporters, interviewers, science, sports and social correspondents, reviewers of books, radio and television programmes, and so on. Illustrations will probably be best done by those who wrote the articles.

The class must also decide on a suitable name, on whether (and how much) to charge for copies and whom to sell them to. School occasions (speech day, exhibition evening, or when there is a concert or play or parents' evening) are often good times to go round selling copies to parents and friends of the school, especially if the profits are going to some charity chosen by the class.

2. Find out what you can about how real newspapers are produced and printed. What jobs do the following men have to do?

editor	crime reporter
sub-editor	special correspondent
news-editor	"our own correspondent"
sports editor	"a correspondent"
feature writer	parliamentary correspondent
leader writer	theatre critic

What is the difference between the various "editions" of a paper? Where should we look to find the views of a newspaper (that is, of its editor) on current issues? Can you list all the leading national daily newspapers at the moment, saying which political party (if any) each usually supports? What local papers are published for your area?

In most libraries, books about newspapers will be classified under the number 070, but you can also use encyclopaedias and other books in the reference section of the library.

3. If possible, arrange for the whole class or a group of pupils to visit a newspaper office and printing works, to see just how the news is handled and printed. If you cannot visit the office of some national paper in the city, try the local newspapers.

Make notes as you go round and prepare a composite article for the class magazine (or a folder, or wall-display) as a record of the visit. The editor of the paper might be interested to see a copy of this himself.

Books To Read

Clarion Call by JAMES STAGG (Dent)
In this book Charles Heston tells his own story: how he made friends with the Weigh family almost in spite of himself, and how they gradually changed his attitude to himself and his disablement, largely by accepting him for what he was, and involving him in their family campaign to save the Heronry.

Devil in Print by MARY DREWERY (Chatto & Windus)
Thomas Warlingham, son of a nobleman of Henry VIII's court, flees to Germany when his father is found guilty of seditious libel against the King. In Cologne he finds employment with a printer at whose shop he meets William Tyndale. Tom returns secretly to England, bringing with him some of Tyndale's Bibles.

A Kind of Secret Weapon by ELLIOTT ARNOLD (Longman)
A 12-year-old boy in Nazi-occupied Denmark becomes involved in the Resistance movement when he discovers his parents printing an underground newspaper—their "kind of secret weapon".

Behind the Scenes on a Newspaper by DUFF HART-DAVIS (Dent)
This is a journalist's description of the whole story of the production of a newspaper, from the work of correspondents and reporters, through the organization of the editorial offices, to the technical processes of printing and reproducing photographs: a fascinating and complex story simply explained by an expert. (Classified as 070.)

Tom is staying with his uncle and aunt in their flat in a large old house. In the hall stands a grandfather clock, which keeps good time, but often strikes the wrong hours. One night Tom is convinced that the clock has struck thirteen, and he goes down to investigate.

CHAPTER THREE

Mystery

The grandfather clock was still there, anyway, and must tell him the true time. It must be either twelve or one: there was no hour between. There is no thirteenth hour.

Tom never reached the clock with his inquiry, and may be excused for forgetting, on this occasion, to check its truthfulness. His attention was distracted by the opening of a door down the hall—the door of the groundfloor front flat. A maid trotted out.

Tom had seen housemaids only in pictures, but he recognized the white apron, cap and cuffs, and the black stockings. (He was not expert in fashions, but the dress seemed to him to be rather long for her.) She was carrying paper, kindling wood and a box of matches.

He had only a second in which to observe these things. Then he realized that he ought to take cover at once; and there was no cover to take. Since he must be seen, Tom determined to be the first to speak—to explain himself.

He did not feel afraid of the maid: as she came nearer, he saw that she was only a girl. To warn her of his presence without startling her, Tom gave a cough; but she did not seem to hear it. She came on. Tom moved forward into her line of vision; she looked at him, but looked through him, too, as though he were not there. Tom's heart jumped in a way he did not understand. She was passing him.

"I say!" he protested loudly; but she paid not the slightest attention. She passed him, reached the front door of the ground-floor back flat, turned the door-handle and went in. There was no bell-ringing or unlocking of the door.

35

Tom was left gaping; and, meanwhile, his senses began to insist upon telling him of experiences even stranger than this encounter. His one bare foot was on cold flagstone, he knew; yet there was a contradictory softness and warmth to this flagstone. He looked down and saw that he was standing on a rug—a tiger-skin rug. There were other rugs down the hall. His eyes now took in the whole of the hall—a hall that was different. No laundry box, no milk bottles, no travel posters on the walls. The walls were decorated with a rich variety of other objects instead: a tall Gothic barometer, a fan of peacock feathers, a huge engraving of a battle (hussars and horses and shot-riddled banners) and many other pictures. There was a big dinner gong, with its wash-leathered gong-stick hanging beside it. There was a large umbrella stand holding umbrellas and walking-sticks and a parasol and an air-gun and what looked like the parts of a fishing-rod. Along the wall projected a series of bracket-shelves, each table-high. They were of oak, except for one towards the middle of the hall, by the grand-father clock. That was of white marble, and it was piled high with glass cases of stuffed birds and animals. Enacted on its chilly surface were scenes of hot bloodshed: an owl clutched a mouse in its claws; a ferret looked up from the killing of its rabbit; in a case in the middle a red fox slunk along with a gamefowl hanging from its jaws.

In all that crowded hall, the only object that Tom recognised was the grandfather clock. He moved towards it, not to read its face, but simply to touch it—to reassure himself that this at least was as he knew it.

His hand was nearly upon it, when he heard a little breath behind him that was the maid passing back the way she had come. For some reason, she did not seem to make as much sound as before. He heard her call only faintly: "I've lit the fire in the parlour."

She was making for the door through which she had first come, and, as Tom followed her with his eyes, he received a curious impression: she reached the door, her hand was upon the knob, and then she seemed to go. That was it exactly: she went, but not through the door. She simply thinned out, and went.

Even as he stared at where she had been, Tom became aware of something going on furtively and silently about him. He looked round sharply, and caught the hall in the act of emptying itself of furniture and rugs and pictures. They were not positively going, perhaps, but rather beginning to fail to be there. The Gothic barometer, for instance, was there, before he turned to look at the red fox; when he turned back, the barometer was still there, but it had the appearance of something only sketched against the wall, and the wall was visible through it; meanwhile the fox had slunk into nothingness, and all the other creatures were going with him; and, turning back again swiftly to the barometer, Tom found that gone already.

(from *Tom's Midnight Garden* by A. Philippa Pearce)

For Discussion

1. Why did Tom feel he ought to take cover when the maid appeared? Why, in fact, was it not necessary?
2. Why did Tom's heart jump?
3. Why did Tom expect the maid to ring the bell or unlock the door when she first passed out of the hall?
4. What words here indicate that Tom had only one slipper on? (He had left the other in the door of his uncle's flat, to stop it from closing.)
5. Why do *you* think the maid made less noise on her second journey through the hall?
6. What is the difference between "positively going" and "beginning to fail to be there" (in the last paragraph)?

37

7. What are, or were, the following?
   a Gothic barometer   a parasol
   an engraving   a ferret
   a wash-leathered gong-stick   a game fowl
8. What do you think had happened in the hall when Tom went down at "thirteen o'clock"?
9. If you find the idea of these stuffed animals unpleasant, explain how the author has given you this impression.
10. Discuss how the author gives this passage a sense of mystery and strangeness. Is Tom really frightened? Would you have been frightened?
11. Do you believe in ghosts, or the possibility of travelling back (or forwards) in time? Could there be any reasonable explanation of Tom's experience?

For Written Answers

1. Why may Tom "be excused for forgetting . . . "?
2. Pick out two adverbs that suggest how mysterious was the fading away of the objects in the hall.
3. Describe (in your own words) the hall as it normally was when Tom knew it.
4. Describe (in your own words) the hall as it seemed to Tom at "thirteen o'clock".
5. Do you think the grandfather clock faded with the other objects? If not, explain why it did not.

The Listeners

"Is there anybody there?" said the Traveller,
  Knocking on the moonlit door;
And his horse in the silence champed the grasses
  Of the forest's ferny floor:
And a bird flew up out of the turret,
  Above the Traveller's head:
And he smote upon the door again a second time;
  "Is there anybody there?" he said.
But no one descended to the Traveller;
  No head from the leaf-fringed sill
Leaned over and looked into his grey eyes
  Where he stood perplexed and still.
But only a host of phantom listeners
  That dwelt in the lone house then
Stood listening in the quiet of the moonlight
  To that voice from the world of men:
Stood thronging the faint moonbeams on the dark stair,
  That goes down to the empty hall,
Hearkening in an air stirred and shaken
  By the lonely Traveller's call.
And he felt in his heart their strangeness,
  Their stillness answering his cry,
While his horse moved, cropping the dark turf,
  'Neath the starred and leafy sky;
For he suddenly smote on the door, even
  Louder, and lifted his head: —
"Tell them I came, and no one answered,
  That I kept my word," he said.
Never the least stir made the listeners,
  Though every word he spake
Fell echoing through the shadowiness of the still house
  From the one man left awake:
Ay, they heard his foot upon the stirrup,
  And the sound of iron on stone,
And how the silence surged softly backward,
  When the plunging hoofs were gone.

WALTER DE LA MARE

Discussing The Poem

1. Can you tell why the Traveller was calling at this place at this time? Can you guess what his business might have been?
2. Which parts of the poem seem particularly effective in suggesting; (a) the silence and solitude of the spot, (b) the dark night, and (c) the frightening air of mystery?

Method Exercises

In Book One we learnt that a full statement sentence requires at least a subject, the person, place or thing that we are talking about, and a verb, a doing or being word, to tell us what is happening. A statement may contain much more, but we expect at least a noun (or pronoun) and a verb. Consider, for example, these two sentences:

1. Corks pop.
2. The corks of champagne bottles usually pop when removed with a corkscrew.

In both, the subject is the noun "corks" and the verb is "pop".

Exercise 1. In the following columns you will find 15 nouns on the left and 15 verbs on the right. The nouns are people, animals, or things which make the noises represented by the verbs, but these are not in the corresponding order.

Pair off the nouns and verbs, and construct *two* sentences for each pair, like the examples 1. and 2. above; one a very short sentence, the other a longer sentence that still uses the same subject and verb.

NOUN	VERB	NOUN	VERB
babies	babble	horses	peal
bells	blare	monks	screech
brakes	boom	pistols	slam
clocks	caterwaul	sleepers	grate
dogs	chant	streams	tick
doors	crack	tom-cats	whine
guns	cry	trumpets	whinny
(rusty) hinges	snore		

As you have probably realised in working out answers to Exercise 1, there is no rule in English to say that the subject must come first in the sentence. Consider these examples from the passage:

> Along the wall projected a series of bracket-shelves, each table-high.

What projected, the wall or the shelves?

> Enacted on its chilly surface were scenes of hot bloodshed.

What were enacted, the surface, the scenes, or the bloodshed?

Exercise 2. What are the subjects of the verbs in the following sentences, all of which have been adapted from the passage? To help you, the verbs have been put in italics.

(a) Tom never *reached* the clock.
(b) His attention *was distracted* by the opening of a door.
(c) Tom *determined* to be the first to speak.
(d) There *were* other rugs down the hall.
(e) The walls *were decorated* with a rich variety of other objects.
(f) In a case in the middle a red fox *slunk* along.
(g) His hand *was* nearly upon the clock.
(h) The Gothic barometer, for instance, *was* there at first.
(i) Meanwhile the fox *had slunk* into nothingness.
(j) All the other creatures *were going* with him.

It is usually easier to pick out the subject word of a statement sentence, but more difficult to spot the subject of a question, command or exclamation sentence. Consider these examples:

All last night the dog was howling.

What kind of a noise was the dog making all last night?

What a noise the dog was making all last night!

Make no noise during the night.

Are the question and the exclamation about the noise or the dog? In order to find the grammatical subject, turn the sentences into the equivalent statement sentences, or the simplest of replies; thus the question becomes:

The dog was making a great noise last night.

The command is more complicated, because we do not usually name the subject at all—it is just "you", that is, whoever we happen to be talking to. It means:

You must make no noise . . .

The subject is therefore "*you* understood", or the name of the person (or animal) commanded.

Exercise 3. Write out the subject of each of the following sentences. Write them in full, with all the adjectives, etc., and then underline the subject word, or *head-word*, of the subject.

e.g. During the last dance, did any young lady in the hall lose a shoe?

Subject: any young lady in the hall.

(a) Has the general's daughter got her shoe back?

(b) How utterly lost the poor travellers felt that night!

(c) George, watch your step with all those parcels!

(d) After a long, delicious meal of soup, roast beef, apple tart, cheese and coffee, the members of the committee no longer felt like discussing their problems.

(e) What is Her Majesty's Government doing about the roads?

(f) Will the main system of motorways be linked to an adequate chain of urban throughways?

(g) My dear friend, please imagine yourself in my position.

(h) What hope has a football club like that?

(i) What did the last lot of tenants pay for their flats?

(j) What a long while the children had to wait!

42

Exercise 4. In the following well-known proverbs we have separated the subjects, in the left-hand column, from the rest of the sentences, on the right, and muddled them. Sort them out so that each subject is placed in its correct sentence and write out the resulting correct proverbs.

e.g. Empty vessels make most sound.

Empty vessels	flock together
Little pitchers	make most sound
Possession	is believing
Pride	may look at a king
A rolling stone	goes before a fall
A bird in the hand	does not make a summer
Birds of a feather	have long ears
A stitch in time	gathers no moss
Too many cooks	are better than one
Silence	is better than no bread
Everybody's business	is worth two in the bush
A friend in need	is nine points of the law
Seeing	is as good as a feast
Two heads	run deep
A cat	is golden
Enough	never boils
Still waters	sweep clean
One swallow	saves nine
New brooms	spoil the broth
Half a loaf	is nobody's business
A watched kettle	is a friend indeed

43

Exercise 5. (a) Here are five *nouns* to do with fear or mystery. What is the difference between the feelings expressed? Can you add at least five more nouns?

shudder   terror   palpitation   qualm   alarm

(b) Here are five *verbs* suggesting fear or mystery. What is the difference between the feelings they represent? Can you add at least five more?

shrink   haunt   horrify   torment   blench

(c) Here are five *adjectives* describing frightening experiences or fearful people. Again, give the meanings and add five more.

hideous   nervous   aghast   eerie   dismal

(d) Here are five *phrases* to do with fear. Again, give the meanings and add five others if you can.

to have cold feet   turn white as a sheet
make someone's flesh creep   make one's teeth chatter
make the blood run cold

(e) Make up five short, vivid descriptions of different terrifying experiences, using some of the words given above, or those that you have collected yourself.

e.g. As I saw the mutilated body lying in the road by the car, my blood ran cold and I blenched, aghast at what had happened. The chill terror seemed to be urging me to turn and run.

Writing Your Own

Study the passage from *Tom's Midnight Garden* again, noting how the author uses many details and a careful choice of words and phrases, to build up a description full of mystery and wonder. The situation is incredible, but the way she tells the story makes it seem real.

There is an art in conveying suspense or mystery in words. Part of the secret is economy: you must not explain too much too soon, but keep the reader uncertain about what is going to happen. Even more important is your choice of descriptive

44

words: those that are always being used ("he was terrified", "it was awful", "you could have knocked him down with a feather") have no real effect on the reader, so you need to find fresh and original words and comparisons. But perhaps most important is your ability to imagine exactly what it would be like, exactly how someone would feel at the terrifying moment, and then to make the reader share these feelings.

Write a ghost story or a short thriller of your own, remembering to try to make it credible, so that anything weird or frightening does seem real and convincing. If you have no good ideas of your own for a plot, then continue the story of Tom in the passage, bringing it to a conclusion of your own invention.

Things To Do

1. Write a poem, expressing strong feelings of terror, horror, disgust or mystery. It will probably be better not to tell a story, but to imagine some vivid incident and concentrate on your feelings and reactions. What flashed through your mind's eye? What did you want to do? What did you feel like, in your stomach, or the palms of your hands, or the roots of your hair? Write simply and directly, going from one word picture to the next as swiftly and simply as the words will let you. This is much more important than worrying about rhyme or rhythm.

Here is an example written by a boy of about your age:

> *Fear*
> The ticking of the clock, the squeaking of the door,
> The hand, then the darkness with no end.
> The patter of footsteps behind you, then
> The thumping in your heart.
>
> The quickening of the pace, the stumble,
> The hand around your neck,
> Then the fingers tightening around your throat;
> Then the waking up.
>
> STEPHEN

The best poems should be selected for publication in the class magazine.

2. Tom's midnight adventures took him back in time about sixty years. Imagine you are able to travel back in time, and prepare, for the class or for the class magazine, an account of a visit to any past age. Use all the reference books you can to help get details correct; the section 942 in most libraries is devoted to British history, and you should look for books like: *London Through the Ages* by Dorothy M. Stuart (Methuen), 942.1. *Growing up in the 13th Century* by Alfred Duggan (Faber), 942.035. *Illustrated English Social History*, 4 volumes, by G. M. Trevelyan (Longmans), 942.

3. Prepare for a debate on the subject *That it is foolish to believe in ghosts*. You will need a chairman to conduct the discussion in an orderly fashion, and a proposer and seconder to prepare speeches (to be given first and third respectively) on one side, and an opposer and seconder of the opposition (to speak second and fourth respectively) on the other. The two seconders prepare shorter speeches, since part of their task is to give answers to the arguments that the proposer or opposer has just put forward. The debate is then thrown open to the rest of the audience to speak (one at a time!), and three minutes before the end the proposer (only) has the right to make a *short final speech*. Then two tellers (or counters of votes), appointed beforehand, count the votes for and the votes against, and the chairman declares the proposal carried or defeated, and adjourns the debate.

Books To Read

Tom's Midnight Garden by A. PHILIPPA PEARCE (O.U.P.; Penguin)
Tom's midnight excursions take him back in time to make
friends with a girl called Hattie who had been lonely in that
house years before. He finds that he is visiting the house and its
beautiful garden at different stages in her life, and only on the
last day of his stay does he discover the secret of his mysterious
adventures.

The Future Took Us by DAVID SEVERN (Penguin)
Peter and Dick suddenly find themselves in the London of A.D.
3000. Britain has been devastated by an explosion, the primitive
people now living there speak a scarcely recognizable language,
and the Calculators and Guards of the Sacred Circle prove
sinister foes.

A Traveller in Time by ALISON UTTLEY (Faber & Faber)
Penelope, visiting her uncle and aunt at the sixteenth century
farm-house, Thackers, strays through a door and finds herself
talking to an Elizabethan aunt kneading dough in an Elizabethan kitchen. At Thackers the Babingtons are supposed to
have lived, and through her dreams Penelope becomes increasingly involved with the family and with the fate of Mary
Queen of Scots.

A Wrinkle in Time by MADELEINE L'ENGLE (Longman; Penguin)
Mrs. Whatsit, the strange visitor in a man's felt hat, a shocking
pink stole, rough overcoat and black rubber boots, arrives
mysteriously one dark, stormy night and sets the Murrys on
the track of their father—an eminent physicist who was lost on
a government mission.

47

Mark and Darkie, a West Indian lad, rescue the mongrel Tuppence from drowning in a London canal, and keep her secretly in a disused shed, even when she has puppies. With the help of the country girl, April, they regularly visit the shed to feed and exercise the dogs.

CHAPTER FOUR

Fog

Looking out of the window the next morning above the net curtain, Mark saw the fog—thick and green, enveloping everything.

"A real pea-souper," said the lodger a little later, waiting for his breakfast in the overcrowded kitchen, watching the fat on the bacon curling crisply in the frying-pan.

Once a fog might have spoiled things, ruined a game in one of the Play Streets, prevented train spotting. But now, thought Mark, walking to Joe's shed, it didn't matter. Tuppence would be there with her welcome; the three puppies would jump against his legs, their tails wagging with mad abandon. He had an interest which filled all gaps, a responsibility which kept him busy, something relying on him.

All over London, muffled by fog, the church bells were ringing, calling people to worship in dim and holy places. Mark thought of Darkie preparing to serve in St. Bartholomew's, of April being dragged to church by her mother, for whom religion was a kind of superstition.

Now and again people carrying torches loomed up suddenly, a blob of light before them, and disappeared as quickly. Mark thought he knew his way by heart along every nearby street. He needed no light.

There were no cars, no buses, no vehicles at all; only the people coming and going and the pealing of the bells. It was eerie.

Mark found the street corner, the turning leading down into the cul-de-sac. He could just distinguish a light here and there breaking through a few feet of fog from a front window. His feet sounded noisy on the empty pavement, sinister, like the beginning of a film. The fog was in his throat and in his lungs. which were not strong. Sometimes he heard people coughing and he imagined they were holding handkerchiefs to their noses, as they had in the time of the great smog some years before. A door slammed and someone shouted, "Hi, Jack, have you seen our Joan?" and then the bells stopped ringing and there was silence. People would be on their knees now, he thought, in the dim light of churches.

He felt in his pocket to make sure he had the opener for the tin of meat April had brought the day before, for the dogs' lunch. Darkie had been earlier to take them for their first run. On Saturdays and Sundays the children would take them out three times.

He came to the turning which was the sentry point and searched the denseness of the fog for the shed. He saw through the green a faint glow and supposed there was a bonfire in the convent's grounds. Fancy adding smoke to the confusion, he thought with annoyance. Bad luck on the puppies. He heard someone running in the distance and wondered how they could see well enough to proceed so fast and then the red glow became stronger and he felt smoke in the back of his throat and smelt it in his nose, dirty and stifling. The glow was in front of him now and it took the form of flames; it crackled and spat out sparks of fire. And it wasn't in the convent's grounds. It was at the end of the road—in Joe's shed. He heard his heart pounding madly and the whine of a dog. He wasn't himself any more but a strange person in a nightmare, this was something which could not happen to Mark Dixon. Coming closer, suddenly deadly calm, he looked more carefully. Smoke was coming out of the window, flames licked up the padlocked door. The whole front was on fire. He had to get round the back. He stumbled over the bit of broken fence, felt his way round and then started to kick the planks, coughing up smoke as he worked. If only he had been wearing his boots . . . but he wasn't. Apart from an occasional splinter his old leather shoes made little impression. He gasped to Tuppence and she barked and he could hear the puppies whimpering. The sound drove him to fresh efforts. He kicked and kicked in vain; the wood held, driving him desperate. He beat with his fists and his hands bled.

(from *The Secret Dog* by Diana Pullein-Thompson)

For Discussion

1. Work out the position of Joe's shed, as far as you can from the evidence in this passage. For instance, about how far was it from Mark's house?
2. Can you suggest a reason why Mark and Darkie kept the dogs in Joe's shed?
3. Why do you think the children had a "sentry point" (mentioned at the beginning of the last paragraph)?
4. How often were the dogs exercised through the week, do you think? Would they be having enough exercise?
5. Is there any hint in the passage that the fire was no accident?
6. What was Mark's first reaction to finding smoke in the air? Is it right to light bonfires in foggy weather?
7. What do the following mean?

responsibility	sinister
preparing to serve	smog
superstition	whimpering

8. Discuss the effect of fog on sounds—what examples does this passage give of these effects?
9. What features of this description show it to be a town fog and not a country one?
10. Why did Mark enjoy looking after the dogs? Do you think he was right to save Tuppence from drowning (they found her with a brick tied round her neck), and to try to save the dogs from this fire?

51

Questions 1, 2 and 3 should each be answered in at least one complete sentence.

1. What kinds of things did Mark used to do on Sundays before he had Tuppence to look after?
2. What did Darkie and April have to do on Sunday mornings?
3. What obstacles had Mark to overcome to save the dogs from the fire?
4. Pick out two adjectives in the first sentence that help to explain why this kind of fog is called a "pea-souper".
5. Pick out examples of description in this passage (not necessarily of fog) appealing to the senses of (a) sight, (b) hearing, (c) smell, (d) taste and (e) touch.

The Fog

Slowly the fog,
Hunch-shouldered with a grey face,
Arms wide, advances,
Finger-tips touching the way
Past the dark houses
And dark gardens of roses.
Up the short street from the harbour,
Slowly the fog,
Seeking, seeking;
Arms wide, shoulders hunched,
Searching, searching.
Out through the streets to the fields,
Slowly the fog —
A blind man hunting the moon.

F. R. McCREARY

Discussing The Poem

1. In what ways is the fog, drifting up from the sea, compared to a man, slowly searching? Are the comparisons appropriate?
2. What is the particular effect of the last line?
3. Discuss the repetition of words and phrases in the poem. Do these have any particular effect?

Method Exercises

What are the subjects of the following sentences, adapted from the passage?

   Mark saw the fog.
   Once a fog might have spoiled things.
   He knew his way.
   He needed no light.
   On Saturdays the children would take them out.
   He heard his heart pounding.

In several cases the subject is "he". What is the name of the person meant by "he"? From Book One, you probably remember that "he" is called a *personal pronoun*. What other personal pronouns can be subjects of verbs?

53

Exercise 1. Write out the subject (often a pronoun) and the verb in each of the following sentences. In some cases there are two subjects.

(a) Mark and Darkie rescued a dog from drowning.
(b) It had a brick tied round its neck.
(c) They took it home with them.
(d) Mark's mother would not have the dog in the house.
(e) At the time she did not want a pet dog.
(f) Afterwards he kept Tuppence in an old shed.
(g) Would you know what to feed a dog on?
(h) He and Darkie took Tuppence tinned food.
(i) I would not like to be shut up all day.
(j) Whenever possible, we should give our dogs plenty of exercise.

Look again at the six sentences on page 53. In the first one, Mark saw something. What did he see? In the second, what might the fog have spoiled? In the others, what did he know? What did he need? What (or whom) would the children take out? What did he hear? The fog, things, way, light and so on are the OBJECTS of the actions—they are seen, are spoiled, are known etc. So we can set the sentences out like this:

SUBJECT		VERB		OBJECT
Mark	—	saw	—	the fog
a fog	—	might have spoiled	—	things
He	—	knew	—	his way

Obviously the difference between subject and object is important; in the second example
Things might have spoiled a fog.
would mean something quite different; and when
The children would take them.
changes to
They would take the children.
the difference is emphasized by the change in the pronouns:
they — them.

54

Exercise 2. Think of suitable objects to complete the following sentences, and rewrite them completed.

(a) At Waterloo, Wellington defeated . . .
(b) Britain, Russia and America fought . . . in the Second World War.
(c) A wheelwright used to make . . .
(d) George Stephenson built . . .
(e) In the play by Shakespeare, Romeo loved . . .
(f) Fog often holds up . . .
(g) In 1492 Columbus discovered . . .
(h) Miss Florence Nightingale founded . .
(i) Elizabeth Fry used to visit . . .
(j) Charles Dickens wrote . . .

Exercise 3. In the following sentences, exchange the subjects for the objects.

     e.g. The chairman selected the committee.
       The committee selected the chairman.

(a) The hero shot the villain through the shoulder.
(b) Every nice girl loves a sailor.
(c) A well-known juvenile delinquent has just struck his father.
(d) You may like your best friend, but I prefer mine.
    (*N.B. 2 verbs here*)
(e) Workers need the new factories.
(f) They used to know us.
(g) Battling Bill defeated Slim Jim in the ring.
(h) You can take your friends home after the party.
(i) The cavalry attacked the troops on the left flank first.

Without looking back at the passage from *The Secret Dog*, discuss where *commas* are necessary in these sentences, and why:

Mark saw the fog—thick and green enveloping everything. He had an interest which filled all gaps a responsibility which kept him busy something relying on him. Someone shouted "Hi Jack have you seen our Joan?" People would be on their knees now he thought in the dim light of churches.

Turn back to see if commas were in fact used where you would have put them, and revise the rule represented by each case. Are there other uses of the comma that were covered in Book One?

Exercise 4. This is a revision exercise on commas. Rewrite the passage inserting the twenty commas that are required.

Fog rolled in from the sea twirling twisting creeping oozing round the buildings facing the sea. Its cold fingers felt the window panes and poked into cracks chinks and crevices through every open window down every chimney under every door. Wet coarse cold choking it breathed into our lungs hung damply on our eyebrows soaked chilly into our garments. Through the dark blank mysterious wall of fog could be heard muffled echoes: a cough footsteps on the stone the distant hoot of ships' sirens. Even the sea seemed cold subdued forlorn.

Exercise 5. Here is a list of nouns representing dwelling places for particular people or animals:

barracks	cote	hive	palace
byre	den	hutch	stable
chalet	drey	igloo	sty
convent	earth	kennel	vicarage
coop	eyrie	manse	warren
			wigwam.

The people or animals appear in a similar list below. Pair them off:

e.g. A king lives in a palace.

American Indian	eagle	king	pig
bees	Eskimo	lion	Scottish minister
cow	fox	nun	soldier
dog	hen	parish priest	squirrel
dove	horse	pet rabbit	Swiss villager
			wild rabbit

Writing Your Own

It might be best to postpone this composition until some foggy or misty weather, when the experience of going out in the fog is fresh in the minds of the class. Make notes first: what does the fog look, smell, feel and taste like? Notice how the cold moisture settles on every twig or blade of grass, as dew or as frost. Watch the way the fog or mist moves and lies. Look up at the street-lights or at the sun or moon—if they are at all visible, they may appear as pale discs or pools of light. Listen to the effect of the fog on the sounds around you, on the traffic and voices and footsteps. Use comparisons as you write (find an example in the passage from *The Secret Dog*). And use your own thoughts, feelings and reactions. (Again, find examples of Mark's thoughts in the passage.)

Write a free verse poem or a composition about a foggy day—here are some suggestions:

Fog at or near the sea.
Fog over a busy town.
Fog on the hills.
Fog by a country river.
An adventure in the fog.
Why I like the fog.
A fire in the fog.
The mists of autumn.

57

Things To Do

1. Make a thorough study of fog, mist, and the precautions that have to be taken against accidents and delays; include the following topics:

The cause of fog.

The differences between fog, cloud and mist.

Parts of the world where fog is common.

Fog signals and equipment at sea.

Fog precautions at airports.

Fog routines on the railways.

Fog precautions on motorways and other roads.

Fog-lamps and fog-horns.

Radar and infra-red devices for path-finding in fog.

Fog and smoke as a danger to health.

Some dramatic fogs of the past.

Some dramatic accidents in past fogs.

2. A dense or prolonged fog should be a suitable news item for the next issue of the class magazine. Reporters could find out the extent of local traffic delays and other disruption caused. Find out how many pupils were late and what school activities had to be cancelled. Some of the information collected by groups or individuals as suggested in No. 1 above would make an interesting background article or articles.

3. A fog should be a good situation for an impromptu play, in which actors would have to mime and act the actions and reactions of different people in a fog. Work out some simple story, perhaps involving a street scene with roadworks, or a market scene, and let the fog add to the confusion and havoc.

Books To Read

The Secret Dog by DIANA PULLEIN-THOMPSON (Collins)
The dog Tuppence set Mark and Darkie a number of problems. Finding food and shelter for her and homes for her puppies was not easy in their overcrowded district of London. She also brought them new friends, especially April; but the gang April had belonged to proved to be new (and unscrupulous) enemies, as well.

We Didn't Mean to Go to Sea by ARTHUR RANSOME (Cape; Penguin)
The "Swallows" are alone aboard the *Goblin* off Felixstowe, for "Captain" Jim Blading has gone ashore and cannot return in the fog that suddenly blankets the coast. On the turn of the tide the anchor drags, and they find themselves at sea in the fog, heading for Holland.

The Weathermonger by PETER DICKINSON (Gollancz; Penguin)
In this book, the first of a science fiction trilogy about the conflict between machines and men, a young boy discovers that he has extraordinary power to control the weather.

The Ivory Anvil by SYLVIA FAIR (Gollancz; Penguin)
A small, anvil-shaped piece from a valuable Chinese puzzle is lost on a Welsh mountainside. Until Sioned can find it, there is a haunting power willing her to search, and carrying her back into the past adventures of old Dinah and the Drowned House.

This is the famous legend of how Troy was captured by the Greeks after they had besieged the city for seven years. Rex Warner has adapted the story from Homer's "Iliad" and other ancient Greek stories.

CHAPTER FIVE

Modern Versions

It was Odysseus who made the plan which was to lead to the fall of Troy. Under his orders the Greeks made out of wood the figure of a huge horse. The face and nostrils of the horse, its feet and hooves were beautifully carved. Its body was hollow and was of such a size that twenty armed men could hide within it. And this is what they did. Odysseus himself with Diomedes, Menelaus, Neoptolemus and others of the best of the Greeks climbed inside the wooden framework of the horse's gigantic body and there they waited fully armed, knowing that this desperate venture would end either in their own deaths or in the destruction of Troy.

For while these great warriors lay hidden inside the horse, Agamemnon, with the rest of the Greek army, had embarked on their ships by night and sailed away. They sailed just as far as the shelter of the island of Tenedos, which lies some twelve miles distant from the Trojan coast. There the fleet was out of sight, and when the dawn came and the Trojan sentries reported that the Greek camp was deserted, all the Trojans believed that their enemies, exhausted and dispirited by their sufferings, had sailed back to Greece, abandoning finally the purpose of their great expedition. It was a day of joy and gratitude in Troy. The people came out of the city, singing and dancing and offering thanks to the gods for what they imagined was their deliverance . . .

When the Greeks had sailed away, they left behind them one man, named Sinon, promising him a great reward and instructing him to tell a false story so that the Trojans would take the horse inside their walls. Now this man Sinon, who had given himself up to a patrol of Trojan soldiers, was brought by them, with his hands tied behind his back, in front of the chief men of Troy. Sinon told his story well. He pretended that he was an enemy of Odysseus and that Odysseus had planned to take his life. Therefore, he said, he had been forced to hide from the Greeks and to throw himself on the mercy of the Trojans. As he spoke of his pretended sufferings, he wept what seemed to be real tears, and there were few who did not believe what he said. As for the horse, he told them that it was an offering which the Greeks had been commanded to make to the goddess Athene. If the Trojans were to destroy it, that would mean certain destruction for their city; but if they took it inside their walls, they would always have the protection of Athene and, in course of time, they would invade Greece itself and conquer the sons or the grandsons of those who had fought against them for so long . . .

So the horse was brought within the walls of Troy and all day the Trojans gave themselves up to feasting and rejoicing. Far into the night their feast continued; no sentries were posted on the walls or along the coast. Confident in their security and tired out from their exertions and their rejoicings, at length they slept in a city that was already almost in their enemies' hands.

For as soon as all was quiet, Sinon made his way to the place where the horse stood. He undid the cunningly contrived bolts, and pulled the timbers apart. Moonlight shone on the eager and expectant faces of the Greeks within, who now gripped their arms, descended from their place of concealment and went quietly through the sleeping city to the gates.

Meanwhile Agamemnon with the whole fleet had set sail from Tenedos. In the silent moonlight they had drawn their ships up on the beach that they knew so well. Silently they had crossed the plain, and now, when Odysseus, Diomedes and the rest opened the city gates to them, they joined forces together and swept into Troy, killing and burning as they went. Almost before the Trojans could arm themselves and long before they could make any plans for defence, the city was lost, high towers were crumbling in ruin and tall flames shooting upwards to the sky. In the moment of their triumph the Greeks showed mercy neither to young nor old Small children and white-haired men were butchered in the streets and in their very beds. So great was the hatred that this long war had provoked, so bitter and outrageous the feelings of those who were at last victorious.

(from *The Fatal Horse* from *Greeks and Trojans* by Rex Warner)

For Discussion

1. Was the story that the horse was an offering to Athene a good one? What made the Trojans believe it?
2. In what ways was Sinon vital to the Greek plan?
3. In what various ways might "this desperate venture" have ended in the deaths of the Greeks inside the horse?
4. What convinced the Trojans of the truth of Sinon's story? Were they very stupid to believe it?
5. Why was the city "already almost in their enemies' hands" as the Trojans went to sleep?
6. Why was it particularly easy for the Greek fleet to return unseen and the men from the horse to open the gates unnoticed?
7. Why do you think the Greeks knew the beach so well?
8. What explanation does the author give for the merciless destruction of Troy by the Greeks? Was such cruelty really justified?
9. Does the fact that the Trojans had been feasting and rejoicing make the end of the story any different?
10. Discuss what the class know of the causes and course of this famous Siege of Troy, and of Homer, who recorded it.

1. Explain how and why the horse was beautifully carved.
2. Explain why the bolts and timbers had to be cunningly contrived.
3. Give the Trojan explanation for the desertion of the Greek camp, in your own words.
4. Describe the city of Troy in your own words, as you imagine it after reading this passage.
5. Describe the scene of destruction as Greeks swept into Troy, again in your own words.

The David Jazz

David was a Young Blood, David was a striplin',
Looked like the Jungle Boy, yarned about by Kiplin' —
Looked like a Jungle Boy, sang like a bird,
Fought like a tiger when his temper got stirred.

David was a-tendin' the sheep for his Pa,
Somebody hollered to him — that was his Ma —
"Run down to camp with this little bitta snack,
Give it to your brothers, an' hurry right back."

David took the luncheon, and off he hurried,
There he saw the Isra'lites lookin' right worried.
Asked 'em what's the matter — they pointed to the
    prairie —
There he saw a sight to make a elephant scary!
There he saw Goliath,
Champion o' Gath,
Howlin' in his anger,
Roarin' in his wrath;
Stronger than a lion,
Taller than a tree —
David had to tiptoe to reach to his knee!

64

"Come on," says the giant, a-ragin' and a-stridin' —
"Drag out your champions from the holes where they're
  hidin',
Drag out your strong men from underneath their bunks,
And I'll give 'em to the buzzards, an' the lizards, an' the
  skunks."

David heard his braggin', and he said, "I declare,
The great big lummox got 'em buffaloed for fair."
Goes to the brook, and he picks him out a pebble,
Smooth as a goose-egg an' hard as the debbil.
Starts for the giant, dancin' on his toes,
Whirlin' his sling-shot and singin' as he goes —
"Better get organized, for here I come a-hoppin',
Time's gettin' short, and hell am a-poppin',
Hell am a-poppin' and trouble am a-brewin',
Nothin's going to save you from Big Red Ruin.
Trouble am a-brewin' and Death am distillin' —
Look out, you Philistine — there's gwine ter be a killin'!"

Giant looks at David an' he lets out a laugh —
Acts like a tiger bein' sassed by a calf;
Laughs like a hyena, grins from ear to ear,
Rattles on his armor with his ten-foot spear,
Starts out for David, bangin' and a-clankin' —
"Come on, l'il infant, you're a-goin' to get a spankin'!"
David takes his sling-shot, swings it round his head,
Lets fly a pebble — and the gi'nt drops dead!

Moral
Big men, little men, houses and cars,
Widders and winders and porcelain jars —
Nothin' ain't safe from damage an' shocks,
When the neighbourhood chillen gets to slingin' rocks!

EDWIN MEADE ROBINSON

Discussing The Poem

1. Find and read the Bible version of this story (I Samuel 17, verses 4–11, 17–27 and 38–51).
2. Discuss any words or phrases in this poem (or in the Bible version) that you do not understand.
3. Consider the ways in which details have been changed in the poem. Why is there talk of "the prairie", "bunks" and "skunks"? What other similar changes of scene have been made, and why?
4. Discuss the title of the poem and the "Moral". What effect do these have on the reader? Is this meant to be a funny story?

Method Exercises

Exercise 1. (a) A large number of *apostrophes* have been used in the poem *The David Jazz* to represent the American negro dialect of English. Nearly all of them are examples of the first rule for the apostrophe in Book One: they represent a letter or letters left out (and not pronounced). Write out the full, correct forms of:

striplin'	o' Gath	Time's	gi'nt
an'	they're	Nothin's	ain't
Isra'lites	hidin'	there's	
'em	I'll	l'il	

(b) In *The Fatal Horse* we find examples of the second rule for the apostrophe, to indicate possession:

the horse's body — the body of the horse

their enemies' hands — the hands of their enemies

Can you remember from Book One this rule for deciding where to put the apostrophe? If not, refer to the footnote at the end of Exercise 5.

What would be the difference in meaning between the following?

> The landlady's prices.

and: The landladies' prices.

How would the following phrases (all adapted from the passage) be rewritten with an apostrophe (as in the examples above)?

the destruction of Troy	the mercy of the Trojans
the shelter of the island	the protection of Athene
the chief men of Troy	the sons of their enemies
the story of Sinon	the expectant faces of the Greeks
the enemy of Odysseus	the feelings of the victors

Exercise 2. Rewrite the following passage, inserting the twenty apostrophes that are required.

"Its uncertain," said the princesss press secretary, "whether her Highnesss engagements will permit her appearance at the St. Pauls Charity Societys Jubilee. In its fifty years history its always enjoyed a royal persons patronage, and its her Majestys wish to continue her familys association with the Societys childrens homes. Shell be delighted," he added, turning to the journalists cameras with a smile, "to see the Presss interest in the St. Pauls childrens homes. The babies happiness depends on the publics generous support."

Exercise 3. We have already seen that in English we do not necessarily begin every sentence with its subject. Good writers vary their sentences as much as possible. Look at the third paragraph of *The Fatal Horse* passage: the main subject and verb of the first sentence is "they left"; of the second, "this man was brought"; of the third "Sinon told".

Each of the following sentences has several main points—in this example they are numbered:

$\overset{1}{\text{They}}$ $\overset{2}{\text{went out, but}}$ $\overset{3}{\text{their parents}}$ $\overset{4}{\text{disapproved.}}$

This might be rewritten:

$\overset{3}{\text{Although their parents}}$ $\overset{4}{\text{disapproved,}}$ $\overset{1}{\text{they still}}$ $\overset{2}{\text{went out.}}$

Or, in another version:

In spite of their parents' disapproval, they still went out. Without leaving points out, rearrange the following sentences, beginning with the opening word or words suggested:

(a) They all spent a day by the sea but the rain ruined it.
    Their day . . .

(b) The match was postponed and the club did not offer any money back.
    In spite of . . .

(c) The stretcher party descended with great care so as not to jolt the wounded climber.
    To avoid . . .

68

(d) He loved to hunt; he loved to ride; he loved to fish; he loved to shoot: these were his chief pleasures.

Hunting . . .

(e) He sacrificed everything so that his daughter might be healthy.

For the sake of . . .

(f) He did not wait for the order to charge, but he thundered down the slope alone.

Without . . .

(g) They knew that this desperate venture might end in death, but they climbed inside the horse.

Knowing . . .

(h) The governors were pleased by the school's success and this led them to declare a half holiday.

The governors' . . .

(i) Some people live in glass houses and those people should not throw stones.

People who . . .

(j) The leader said something to his men and this fired them with new enthusiasm.

What the leader . . .

Exercise 4. We have noticed before that writers frequently use comparisons to describe people, things and actions. Find comparisons in *The David Jazz* to tell us how David fought, how smooth and hard the pebble was, and how the giant acted when faced with David. These comparisons, using the words *like* and *as*, are called SIMILES. (Make sure you learn to pronounce this word correctly.) The writer's aim is to use something familiar in order to describe something more strange, unusual or special. On the other hand, if the comparison itself becomes too familiar, we accept it without thinking, and it does not really describe at all. Thus:

> Johnny was as good as gold.

no longer helps describe how good he was. And:

> He ran as fast as anything.

is almost meaningless!

But to talk of:

A line of elms plunging and tossing like horses.

is lively, vivid, unusual and yet extremely appropriate.

Complete the following sentences with the most original, interesting and appropriate similes you can think of:

(a) The angry Greeks fell on their enemies like . . .
(b) The bare branches of the trees stretched towards the sky like . . .
(c) The old man's face was as withered and wrinkled as . . .
(d) She danced as lightly and gaily as . . .
(e) The ruined church, jagged against the cold winter's sky, was like . . .
(f) The atmosphere in the hall was welcoming, warm and friendly: it was like . . .
(g) The cobweb, glistening with frost, was like . . .
(h) The old woman moaned like . . .
(i) He was always as charming as . . .
(j) The new office block, towering above us, was . . .

Exercise 5. (a) On the left below you will find a list of nouns and a list of adjectives. Pair them off so that they are all suitably matched. On the right are lists of verbs and adverbs: again, pair them off.

e.g.   ceaseless chatter | wear out completely

NOUN	ADJECTIVE	VERB	ADVERB
chatter	expensive	wear out	noiselessly
roar	powerful	disturb	deftly
climbers	melancholy	ascend	uproariously
candles	excited	flicker	peacefully
children	melting	laugh	insufferably
grandmother	hopeful	dream	solemnly
jewels	graceful	glitter	mightily
suitors	skilful	pester	temptingly
swans	serene	float	uncertainly
giant	deafening	heave	increasingly
mourners	ceaseless	walk	completely

(b) Now compose for each of your answers a sentence using the noun (with its adjective) as subject and choosing an appropriate tense of the corresponding verb (and adverb):

e.g. Their ceaseless chatter wore us out completely.

Footnote: The rule for using the apostrophe to show possession is as follows:
Add an apostrophe to the noun naming the owner of some thing or quality, then add an -s, unless the noun already ends in a *single* -s.
e.g. men's suits; girls' shoes; the boss's car; the foreman's office.
This rule works with only a few exceptions, e.g. "bus's" and proper names such as "St. Thomas's."

Writing Your Own

The passage and the poem in this chapter are two very different ways of telling a story, not simply because one is in prose and the other a poem. Both are well-known and ancient stories, but while one has been told simply and clearly, with the main emphasis on what happened, the other is retold as if it happened very recently and (for the American negroes) in their own part of the world. In this second story the two main people are given great life and importance: they have likely, lively things to say. And in the second story, although it was a serious enough event at the time, there is an element of light-heartedness and humour.

In both stories, however, the arrangement and paragraphing are important. Study the paragraphs in the story *The Fatal Horse* and give each a title to describe what it is mainly about. What is the equivalent of paragraphs in the verse story? Equally important is the building up of effects or the description of characters. To make the story of David and Goliath effective, it is essential to create an impression of David as a mere lad, inexperienced and weak, but curiously brave and impatient of his elders, and of Goliath as enormous, terrifying, superbly armed and very over-confident. Show how the poem (or the Bible version) achieves this.

71

Write a short story. If you wish, retell some well-known tale from history or legend. Or, alternatively, "modernize" and adapt some such story, or make up a plot of your own. Here are some suggestions:

> Samson and Delilah.
> A tale of Robin Hood.
> One of the labours of Hercules.
> The death of Julius Caesar.
> Alfred and the burning of the cakes.
> How the elephant got his trunk.
> A modern tale with a moral.
> A story of King Arthur.
> The story of Noah and the Flood.

Things To Do

1. Find out what you can about the characters mentioned in *The Fatal Horse* (Odysseus, Menelaus etc.), about Homer, his *Iliad*, and about the whole Trojan War. Use reference books such as:

> *The Oxford Companion to Classical Literature.*
> *Lempriere's Classical Dictionary.*
> *The Oxford Junior Encyclopedia, Vol. I, Mankind.*
> *A Classical and Biblical Reference Book* by H. A. Treble (Murray).

You will need to understand the meaning of *q.v.*, and be prepared to look up the information under various headings.

2. Work out a mime or an impromptu dramatization of either *The Fatal Horse* or *The David Jazz*. The story of the Wooden Horse should offer a wide variety of very different characters to act, and you will have to be ingenious to work out an effective way of showing the horse itself, and the men inside—perhaps some construction of desks and chairs would do.

3. Some of the short stories written by the class should be useful contributions to the class magazine. As a variation on short stories, an individual or a group could work on a serial story in several parts. Careful planning will be necessary, and it is important to end each episode at an exciting point so that readers will want to buy the next issue to read what happens next.

Books To Read

Greeks and Trojans by REX WARNER (Heinemann)
The author retells the story of all the main episodes of the Trojan War in a clear (and exciting) modern English version, from the founding of Troy and the judgement of Paris to the deaths of Hector and Achilles and the sack of the city.

The Gorgon's Head and *The Way of Danger* by IAN SERRAILLIER
    (O.U.P.; Heinemann)
These are both books about Greek heroes. The first is the story of Perseus, and of the head of Medusa that turned all things to stone. The second is the life of Theseus, from his adventurous journey to find his father, King of Athens, to his death by treachery.

The Ivory Horn by IAN SERRAILLIER (O.U.P.; Heinemann)
This book retells the story of Roland, nephew to the Emperor Charlemagne, who fought and died heroically in the struggle against the pagan armies in Spain in the 8th century.

A Book of Myths by ROGER LANCELYN GREEN (Dent; Dutton)
This is a book of stories from the ancient civilizations of the Middle East, not re-told before: strange tales of gods, creation, war and adventures in life and after death. This author has re-written a number of other mythical tales, many published by Puffin books.

Lincoln, Miranda and Pinks arrive first, straight from boarding school, at the furnished house where they are to spend Christmas, and they are cut off by winter floods before their parents can join them. Without electricity or telephone and with only a little food, they battle with the swirling waters, give shelter to a local shepherd and his family, and (with the help of Oliver Cromwell, the bull terrier) rescue a ewe and her lambs.

CHAPTER SIX

Christmas

It was the strangest Christmas they had spent and yet one of the most happy. No mail van halted at the door with parcels and cards. At breakfast there were no gifts to unwrap with paper drifted round the table legs. They couldn't hurry to church clad in new fur-backed gloves and head-scarves, and sing carols, with shaggy gold chrysanthemums scenting the air and holly berries squashed between the flag-stones in the aisle. Instead, there was *Little Topsails* with its trampled floors, the ever-hungry animals, and the needs of the family who had come to them for shelter.

Miranda and the others were all tired. They felt as if they had been swimming for a long time in a rough, buffeting sea. All they needed to do was to keep on a little; yet it was just this last effort which seemed so hard.

"Tom Hunter says his wife is a wonderful cook," Lincoln remarked to Miranda as he laid the breakfast table. "Even if they have to stay another day or two he doesn't want you to worry. She'll manage however short we are of food."

Miranda didn't look up. She was cooking an omelette which had stuck to the frying pan because there hadn't been enough butter to grease it properly. For some reason she didn't even understand herself she felt angry with Lincoln. A hot tear slid down her cheek and tumbled into the pan.

"I don't mind how long they have to stay," she said, "but I hope she won't interfere. We've managed by ourselves so far and I'd rather do it now to the end."

"Of course she won't," said Lincoln. "She'll be busy seeing to what clothes they have left, and the baby. It's only that she's there to ask if you're stuck."

And Mrs. Hunter didn't interfere. She seemed to understand how Miranda felt about housekeeping far better than her own brother . . .

There was too much to do to linger out of doors. Tom Hunter set out to try and salvage some of his possessions from the wrecked caravan, and Miranda was soon closeted with his wife, who had promised to help her with the rabbit and the Christmas pudding.

"Stewed it should go a fair way," she told Miranda after they had skinned the rabbit and left the joints to soak in salted water. "And there should be just enough fruit for the pudding. In my purse I've the silver threepenny bit we put in ours. You're welcome to pop it in, wrapped round in greaseproof paper."

"And I've my silver thimble," said Miranda, "and Pinks has the button from last year."

While the house filled with the scent of cooking Pinks and her brother dragged rugs and carpets to dry on the terrace, threw open the windows to air the rooms, and lit a fire in the sitting-room. Of all the Christmas tree decorations only the fairy doll remained, and a single scarlet glass ball which had floated to safety in the log basket.

"We'll use the ball in a holly garland to hang on the front door," decided Pinks. "Then it will be the very first thing they'll see."

Everything they did that morning was in preparation for their parents' arrival. They worked very hard as if the fact of having everything ready would speed their coming . . .

The house was full of the sound of scrubbing and brushing. They used every brush they could find, even the hard broom from the stable. They polished the grandfather clock and the oak staircase, and Pinks burnished every brass door knob. They cleaned the windows and swept the floors till the last grain of mud had disappeared.

By half-past twelve everything was ready. The long table in the kitchen was spread with a white cloth and polished silver. The black olives, the football biscuits, preserved ginger, and

76

Gorgonzola cheese were all set out. The rabbit was cooked and the pudding steamed in its basin in the double saucepan. At the head of the table Pinks had laid places for their mother and father.

"I'm sure they'll come in time for lunch," she declared. "We can't begin without them."

(from *Castaway Christmas* by Margaret J. Baker)

For Discussion

1. How did Miranda feel about housekeeping?
2. Why do you think Miranda felt angry with her brother? Was she justified in feeling angry, and if so, should she have been angry with *him*?
3. Did she in practice let Mrs. Hunter help? If so, how?
4. What was the name of the house? List all the "ever-hungry animals".
5. What supplies do you imagine had already been sent for their Christmas, before the flood marooned them, and how much of these survived the flood?
6. What simile is used to show how tired they were? Is it appropriate and effective?
7. What were they going to have for their Christmas meal? What seems to be missing, by normal standards?
8. In what other ways is this "castaway Christmas" contrasted with a normal one?
9. Can you give examples of adults less tactful than Mrs. Hunter trying to "help" you? Is it always right for them to interfere when they know they can do better?
10. What seems to you most important about keeping Christmas—(a) the religious element, going to traditional church services, and so on; or (b) the giving of presents and the traditional good things to eat and drink; or (c) the opportunity for families to meet together at least once a year?

1. Where were Mr. and Mrs. Hunter living before the flood?
2. What evidence is there in the passage that the ground floor of the house had also been flooded?
3. How did the children deal with the aftermath of the flood?
4. What kind of persons do you imagine (a) Lincoln, (b) Miranda, and (c) Mrs. Hunter to be?
5. Explain in your own words why they worked so hard, when they were tired and expected help in any case.

Method Exercises

Look at this extract adapted from the passage:

"Stewed it should go a fair way," she told Miranda. "And there should be just enough fruit for the pudding. In my purse I've the silver threepenny bit we put in ours. You're welcome to pop it in, wrapped round in greaseproof paper."

Suppose it were punctuated and set out like this:

"Stewed it should go a fair way," she told Miranda. "And there should be just enough fruit for the pudding."
"In my purse I've the threepenny bit we put in ours."
"You're welcome to pop it in, wrapped round in grease-proof paper."

Explain clearly what difference this would make to the meaning: who is now offering the threepenny bit? Correct punctuation and setting out are clearly important.

Now examine these two examples, adapted from the passage:

"I don't mind how long they have to stay," she said, "but I hope she won't interfere."

"Of course she won't," said Lincoln. "She'll be busy seeing to what clothes they have left."

Why is there a small "b" after "she said", but a capital "S" after "said Lincoln"?

A full stop and capital letter would also be required if the first sentence spoken ended in a question mark or an exclamation mark:

> "Have you finished yet?" asked George. "We are in a hurry."

> "Nonsense!" Peter replied angrily. "We have plenty of time."

Notice that the question mark and exclamation mark come inside the inverted commas (since George spoke a question and Peter an exclamation), and that they replace the comma that was used in the earlier examples.

Exercise 1. Rewrite the following conversation putting in all the punctuation (including one apostrophe). Paragraphing and capital letters are already correct.

> Do you think that one will do said Joyce as they looked at the pile of glass balls on the counter

> Which one asked Pat The red one or the blue or the green

> Silly replied Joyce I didnt mean any particular one I meant one as opposed to two or three

> Oh in that case Pat laughed you should say what you mean

> I did say what I meant Joyce said firmly If I had meant what you thought I had meant she continued I would have asked whether you thought that *that* one would do

Exercise 2. (a) Discuss the following five differently punctuated versions of the same nine words. How should each be pronounced when read aloud? What differences in meaning are there between them?

 i. "What! Do you think he replied with a smile?"
 ii. "What do you think?" he replied with a smile.
 iii. "What do you think! He replied with a smile."
 iv. "What do you think?"
     He replied with a smile.
 v. "What? Do you think?" he replied with a smile.

(b) See how many different versions you can make of the following sentences, simply by altering the punctuation (do not add or omit any words). When every member of the class has made his or her own attempt, pool all the different suggestions, checking that they all make sense.

 i. why did he go to discover the truth
 ii. how do you know he answered frankly
 iii. he said I said it was not true
 iv. I know he thought too much
 v. what she said was the reply they suggested

Study this extract, adapted from a dictionary.

slight *a.* slim, slender, frail-looking;
    not substantial; trifling.
  v. to disregard; to neglect.
  n. indifference; an act of discourtesy.
  slightly *adv.* not greatly, to a slight degree.
slim *a.* thin, slight; crafty. (-ly, *adv.*; -ness, *n.*)
  v. to make (oneself) thin.
slime *n.* sticky mud; sticky fluid.
  slimy *a.* covered with slime; slippery. (-ily, *adv.*;
  -iness, *n.*)

What do the abbreviations *a., n., v., adv.* mean? Why are some of the words in bold type not against the left-hand margin? Why is there a comma after "slender", but semicolons after "frail-looking" and "not substantial"?

Exercise 3. (a) Using the dictionary extract on Page 80, identify the exact meaning and use of the words in italics in the following sentences; for example, the first one is:

"slight"—adjective (describing "man") meaning "frail-looking".

Number the others 1 to 10:

The father was a *slight* man, old, careworn, with a *slight* stammer. I knew him *slightly*, but when his *slim* figure appeared on the balcony, and he did not greet me, I felt sure it was a deliberate *slight* or snub. Indeed, the whole family *had slighted* us at every *slight* opportunity. My sister might have been something that had crawled out of the *slime* to them. When she slipped once on the *slimy* jetty by their boathouse, John, the tall, *slim* one, turned his head *slightly* and then walked away.

(b) Answer the following questions about the dictionary extract:

  i. Is there an adverb formed *directly* from "slime"?

 ii. What are the abstract nouns formed from "slight", "slimy" and "slim"?

iii. What is the less common meaning of "slim"?

(c) Compose one sentence using *slim* as a verb and another using *slime* in its second meaning.

Exercise 4. (a) Study this short business letter. George wanted the catalogue of model kits so that he could choose some suitable ones to give as Christmas presents.

110, Goldings Road,
NAPEBURY,
Leicestershire,
LE5 3AT
4th December, 19—.

Stickwell Models, Ltd.,
Borough Road,
Ealing,
London, W13C 2FD
Dear Sirs,

Would you please send me a free catalogue and price-list of all your model kits, both Series A and Series B ?

I am particularly interested in your special Christmas offer of Double-one kits as advertised in the "Young Modeller" last week.
Yours faithfully,
George Weekly.

It is usual to put both addresses at the top of a business letter. Can you think of any good reasons for this? Why did George start the letter "Dear Sirs," instead of "Dear Sir" or "Dear Stickwell Models" or "Dear Mr. Stickwell"? Why did George add his second paragraph? How will Stickwell Models know where to send the catalogue? Notice how the addresses and the date are set out and punctuated, and also the correct way to end a business letter.

(b) Set out the following business letter correctly, with all the necessary punctuation. (Jean is going to spend a week in London after Christmas.)

14 blockford lane cressingford gloucestershire gl8 7q3 30th november 19— the public relations officer london transport 55 broadway london sw1e 6rj dear sir please could you send me a copy of the booklet visitors london together with a set of free london transport maps I enclose a postal order for 25p and trust that this will cover the cost and postage yours faithfully jean cousins

82

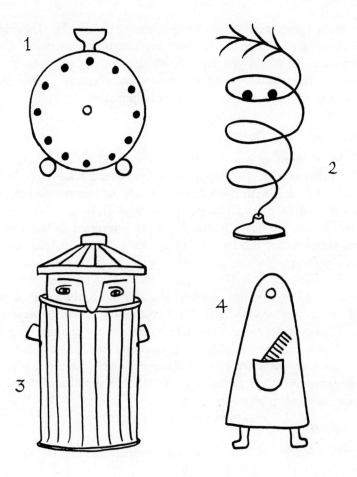

Exercise 5. The drawings above are whatever you like to think they are. For instance number 1 might be a clock that has just said, "Hands off my face!" or it might be the front view of a wheelless steam engine, a mishandled teapot that has ceased to spout, or a view of the round-eared, one-eyed stickabat, hanging upside down. This last creature uses its round ears for listening in all directions and therefore only needs one eye. It attaches itself to its prey by the sucker on its head and then sucks out the meat it lives on.

83

Write your own account (or accounts) of the drawings on page 83. Try to make your explanations both witty and improbable. When you have finished these, try drawing your own pictures and writing accompanying accounts. Make the pictures simple and the accounts complicated.

Writing Your Own

1. What seem to you the most exciting and satisfying aspects of Christmas? Do you enjoy the shops, overflowing with light and piled high with good things for sale, or the decorations at home and in public places, bright and glowing in the cold December evenings? Or are you more interested in the active preparations for the festival, in all the cooking, making cards and presents, putting up decorations, preparing for parties, and so on? Or is it the religious plays and services, the old stories told once more, on television and radio, the warm sense of beauty and goodwill and holiness that you can experience at Christmas? Or perhaps Christmas simply means to you what you can get out of it—rich food and drink, and plenty of presents, and you are cynical about the whole business. Whatever your view, try to express it fully, with detail and description, in a composition entitled:

WHAT CHRISTMAS MEANS TO ME.

2. Write ONE of the following business letters, using the example on page 82 as a model.

(a) Answer the following imaginary advertisement:
HELP FIGHT POVERTY with your
CHRISTMAS CARDS this year. Write
for a free catalogue of these
delightful cards, specially drawn
for us by world-famous artists, to
WORLD CAMPAIGN AGAINST POVERTY
35 Martian's Row, Glasgow G22 3AW,
and help the poor help themselves
this Christmas.

84

(b) A letter to accompany a cheque for £6-63 which your class has raised by selling its class magazine, to the St. Boniface Home for Handicapped Children, St. Boniface House, East Lane, Oxbridge, Buckinghamshire, SL6 2AP. The class have unanimously voted to give the money to this home.

(c) Ask a store in your nearest large town to deliver a particular article which you want to give as a present. Find the address in a telephone book. Describe the article very clearly by its correct trade name, with any necessary details about size, and, of course, say you enclose a postal order to cover cost and delivery or postage.

Things To Do

1. A Christmas number of the class magazine will be an excellent way of raising money for some charity this Christmas. The class should suggest possible good causes and vote on which to choose.

The magazine should have a special Christmas cover, and the contents should have a Christmas flavour: plenty of light-hearted material, puzzles and games suitable for the season, articles and stories on Christmas themes (for instance, hints on Christmas parties, and so on).

A school play, concert, exhibition or parents' party would be an excellent opportunity to sell copies to parents and friends of the school.

2. Make a selection of Christmas poems and unusual carols. Include some of your own original verse and illustrations. This could be a class anthology, brought together and bound in a folder; or an individual one, representing your own taste and skill.

3. Try to write a Christmas carol of your own, either to a tune of your own composition, or using some well-known tune that you think suitable, and fitting words to it. Several people might co-operate to compose a carol between them.

4. Do you have candles at home at Christmas? Either at home or at school, study a burning candle: an ordinary, cheap white candle will do, and it is not difficult to arrange to burn a dozen of these round the class-room on saucers. Study the flame and the wax closely: does the flame reach to the bottom of the wick? Is the flame the same colour throughout? How does it react to a draught or a vibration of the desk? What shapes does the flame take? What happens to the melting wax? Is there smoke or shimmering air above the candle? What happens when you put the flame out? Make notes first, and then work these into a poem or a piece of descriptive prose; here is an example by a pupil:

The Candle Flame

It is still, reaching and pointing.
   Then, sitting above the candle
It begins, jumping, quivering and dancing.
   Smoking, flickering and prancing.

Sometimes like a fir-cone,
   Squat, bulbous and motionless;
Sometimes like a tower,
   Tapering, reaching and pointing.

Then it flinches back and quivers,
   And the small, golden flame disappears.
Extinguished!
   Its only remnant being a thin spiral of smoke,
Whispering, spindling, spiralling away.

STEPHEN

86

Books To Read

Castaway Christmas by MARGARET J. BAKER (Methuen; Penguin)
The passage in this chapter was taken from near the end of the
swift-moving and dramatic story of how the Ridley children
coped with their alarming adventure.

The Village That Slept by MONIQUE PEYROUTON DE LADEBAT
(translated by Thelma Niklaus) (Bodley Head)
A girl, a boy and a baby wake up on a desolate mountain with
no memories of their previous life. Hungry and cold, they
struggle to a nearby village, but are shattered to find it deserted.
When they can find no way out over the mountains, they set
up home in a house with a few supplies, and try to keep themselves alive and cheerful as they await rescue.

The Year of the Wolves by WILLI FÄHRMAN (O.U.P.)
The fifth Christmas of the Second World War, in 1944, passed
normally on the Bienmanns' farm in East Prussia. But the
Germans were retreating, the family would soon be uprooted,
and the chaos and terror at the end of the war would bring out
the beast, the wolf, in many people.

Hills End by IVAN SOUTHALL (Angus and Robertson; Penguin)
Seven children, a school-mistress and the man at the saw-mill
are left cut off from all help by a terrible storm that wrecks the
town. How they manage to survive dangers and difficulties
until relief comes makes a gripping and unusual story.

This is an account of the Pilgrim Fathers, who were among the first settlers of New England. This part of the story is told by Giles Hopkins, a lad of fifteen, who has been asked to keep up William Bradford's journal while he is too ill to do so himself.

CHAPTER SEVEN

A Diary

Tuesday, January 9, 1621

A reasonable fair good day. Everyone is hopping busy. We went to labour in the building of our town. We are building the houses in two rows for more safety. There is to be a street between named Leyden after a city in Holland where some have lived. Only the plots, measured at three poles length, have been marked out, as all must work on the Common House first. Our house will be to the South Side of the brook, facing woodwards, which pleases me.

Some worked to-day at the sawing of logs and some split them into clapboards. I sawed, that taking less skill. For sawing we have dug a great pit in the frozen ground. A log is put over it and one man gets into the pit and one stays above, thus we pull the saw back and forth, yet it is not very easy. I was paired off with John Billington half this day. We spoke little. John does not quarrel with me now, yet he seems to regard me as a rival. Never once did he stop the sawing, hoping I think, to wear me out, which he almost did, though my pride kept me going. Sometimes he seems almost friendly, I do not understand him.

Wednesday, January 10

While wandering inland at noontime, Robert Carver, a servant to the Mullens, came upon more buried corn. Mother has pleased everyone much by mashing the corn into a batter and boiling it together with spring water and Arabella's milk. Mother has named the dish "hasty pudding", because it takes no time in making. Very good it is, like mush.

We worked on at the building, arm weary by evening, even the men.

Thursday, January 11

William Bradford is still ill of pain in his hucklebone—the rheumatic fever, says Dr. Fuller, who has kept hot stones from the hearthboy on him for three days.

While felling trees, Edward Doty, one of our servants mislaid a broadaxe, which much disturbed Gilbert Winslow, who is a carpenter and pleased by all tools. With tools we are not too well supplied, having only arm-saws, hand saws, long axes, hand hatchets, three augers, two crowbars, and three sledges. I am still on the arm-saw with Billington, though later I hope to wield a sledge and thereby build up my muscles. Worked all day, without any notable occurrences. No Indians to be seen.

Friday, January 12

Governor Carver has ordered that each of the nineteen houses to be built shall be done by the men who live in them, thinking by that course we will, out of friendly rivalry, make more haste than by building in common. A stockade is to be built around the whole colony. Governor Carver has placed his house in the middle.

Father was much troubled with sciatica to-day and stayed on shipboard with Oceanus. Mother worked ashore, dividing her time between gathering thatch and washing clothes. Sister Constance helped her, while Damaris busied herself trying to aid them both, though being barely five years old she hindered them rather more than she helped.

The sun beamed out warm this afternoon and mother thought much of seeding time.

Saturday, January 13

The Common House was near finished to-day, wanting only half its covering. In four days half of it has been thatched and mortared. The chimney of wet clay is plastered up with sticks but not yet ready for the fire. Some of the sick, including William Bradford, have moved from the ship to the Common House, there better to see our progress and to have their needs administered to without breaking our work.

Frost and foul weather came this afternoon and hindered us mightily. On a hill not so far distant, we saw a fire burning. Captain Standish climbed a tree the better to view the fire and to see if there were Indians around it. He saw nothing, and came down greatly disappointed. He feels the savages are all about us, watching, but too wary yet to show themselves.

(from *Mayflower Boy* by Stanley Young)

For Discussion

1. What do you imagine a "clapboard" to be?
2. Why was sawing easier than splitting? Do you think working the saw from the pit would be easier than sawing from above?
3. As far as you can, describe each of the tools mentioned. What would we call an "arm-saw"? And were "sledges" tools or means of transport?
4. How do you imagine the Common House was constructed?
5. Oceanus was a baby only a few weeks old. Can you suggest why he was given this name?
6. Explain the treatment that Dr. Fuller recommended for William Bradford.
7. How do we know from this passage that the ship was still anchored nearby? Was it of any help to the settlers to have the ship at hand?
8. At what season do you think they had arrived from Europe? Why had the ship not already returned across the Atlantic?
9. Who, do you think, buried the corn?
10. Why was Captain Standish "disappointed"?
11. What do you know about the Pilgrim Fathers? How was it that some of them had lived in Leyden? (Where is Leyden?)
12. What features of the way this is written are typical of a diary? Why do diary-writers frequently leave out the pronoun "I"?

For Written Answers

1. What was the Hopkins' goat's name?
2. Why did Giles want to build up his muscles?
3. Explain why the tools were so precious to the settlers.
4. Describe the site they had chosen for their settlement, as far as we can tell from this passage.
5. List the various precautions the settlers took for their safety. What were they anxious to be protected from?

Method Exercises

> *Everyone* is busy.
> *We* went to labour.
> *Some* have lived in Holland.
> *All* must work on the Common House.
> The site of our house pleases *me*.

Each of these sentences (adapted from the passage) includes a *pronoun*. What person(s) or thing(s) does each pronoun stand for? Notice that some are singular and some plural, and that some have different forms for subject or object. As a reminder, here are the *personal pronouns* that were discussed in Book One.

	SUBJECT	OBJECT
Singular	I	me
	you	you
	he	him
	she	her
	it	it
Plural	we	us
	you	you
	they	them

In addition, the following *singular* pronouns are found as subject *or* object:

> each, everyone, none, no one, nobody, one, this, that, some, another.

And the following *plural* pronouns can also be subject *or* object:

> all, both, these, those, some, others.

Exercise 1. In the following passage about the settlers, twenty pronouns are in italics. State whether each is subject or object, singular or plural, and what it refers to:

e.g. We—subject, plural, refers to the settlers.

We are busy building the Common House and *all* must work to finish *this* first. *I* work with John and my pride keeps *me* going. *He* is sometimes friendly, but *I* do not understand *him*. *Everyone* has to help *others* in this work. *Nobody* is allowed to be lazy.

Mother has made a new pudding. *It* is very tasty and *everyone* likes *it*. *She* called *it* "hasty pudding" and *none* of it was wasted on the men: *they* all wanted *some* and praised *her* for inventing *it*.

Exercise 2. The following statements have been taken from the passage. Most of them are true sentences in that they have a subject and a verb—write these out, as in the following example:

　Everyone is hopping busy
　Subject—everyone; verb—is.

But three of them are incomplete; in these cases rewrite the sentences, adding the necessary subject or verb or both, and then write out the subject and verb in the same way.

(a) A reasonable fair good day.
(b) I sawed, that taking less skill.
(c) We spoke little.
(d) Very good it is, like mush.
(e) Worked all day, without any notable occurrences.
(f) No Indians to be seen.
(g) A stockade is to be built around the whole colony.
(h) Mother worked ashore, dividing her time between gathering thatch and washing clothes.
(i) In four days half of it has been thatched.
(j) On a hill not far distant, we saw a fire burning.

In the dictionary extract in the last chapter (page 80), *slight* as an adjective was said to mean *slim* or *slender*. These three adjectives are very similar in meaning. Words of similar meaning are called SYNONYMS. What two synonyms did that dictionary extract give for *slim*, and what one for *slimy*? Synonyms, however, are not always identical in meaning: slippery things are not always slimy—think of an example to show this, and discuss the subtle difference in meaning.

Exercise 3. With the help of a dictionary, find synonyms (as many close ones as you can) for:
>tall, clever, small, strong, old, (all adjectives);
>edge, man, teacher, flag, beginning, (all nouns);
>plunge, jump, slip, annoy, talk, (all verbs).

Exercise 4. Rewrite the following sentences, choosing the most suitable word to complete the sentence from the synonyms given in brackets.
>e.g. The falling saucepans made a great
>(*clatter*, roar, uproar, hubbub, blare).

(a) Joan of Arc was (inflamed, roasted, burned, singed) at the stake.
(b) The magician waved his (rod, stick, wand, staff, bar) and the rabbit appeared.
(c) His jacket was (sullied, stained, tarnished, tainted) with ink.
(d) He was inclined to (peek, peep, peer, pry) into other people's business.
(e) The old-fashioned way of making bread involves (massaging, rubbing, kneading, stroking, manipulating) the dough.
(f) The third (shake, quiver, flutter, ripple, tremor) of the earthquake was the worst.
(g) Iron-ore is smelted in a (blast furnace, fire-box, crematorium, kiln, oven, incinerator).
(h) In the fourth round, after being severely cut over one eye, the Slasher (conceded, admitted, confessed, avowed) the victory to his opponent.

94

(i) First one has to remove the (peel, crust, bark, skin, rind, husk, shell) of the bananas.

(j) He tried to pass some (mock, sham, spurious, counterfeit, artificial) money over the shop counter, and was accused of (fabrication, forgery, invention, fraud, falsification).

Can you say what slightly different meanings the other synonyms in each of these lists have?

Exercise 5. Here is a letter that Michael wrote to his uncle, Joseph Johnson, at 17, Peg Hill, Polesby, Yorkshire, DN16 2PD.

> *12, Lace Lane,*
> *Peckham,*
> *London, SE15 2EU*
> *9th January, 19—*

Dear Uncle Joe,

Mother is going into hospital tomorrow, Friday, rather earlier than we expected, and Dad hopes you will not mind if he does not bring Grandma and me up by car tomorrow. He wants to be in London so that he can visit Mother over the weekend. He is planning to drive us up to Euston and put us on the Yorkshire Flyer in the morning. We should reach Polesby at 6.30 in the evening, all being well.

Could you please meet us with the car at the station? We shall have quite a lot of luggage and, of course, Grandma's wheel-chair, and would be grateful for the help.

We are both looking forward very much to our stay. We all send our love.

> *Yours,*
> *Michael.*

(a) Imagine that, in the rush of getting Mother ready for hospital and himself and Grandma ready for the trip to Yorkshire, he had time only for a brief postcard to explain the situation. Write the postcard, remembering that you can shorten the address and date to save space.

(b) Imagine now that it was already early on the 10th January when they decided to go by train. Uncle Joe has no telephone. Make up the shortest possible telegram to send before Michael leaves for Euston. In the illustration you will see a typical telegram form.

How much would your telegram cost?

Counter No................				Serial No..	
Office Stamp				Chargeable words	Sent at/By
	POST ♕ **OFFICE**				
	INLAND TELEGRAM			Charge	Circulation
	FOR POSTAGE STAMPS				
	For conditions of acceptance, see over				
	Prefix	Handed in	Service Instructions	Actual words	
If you wish to pay for a reply insert **RP** here	**To**	BLOCK LETTERS THROUGHOUT PLEASE			

SAMSON'S CIRCUS, HIGH COMMON,
BERKHAMFIELD, BUCKS.

CHAMPION FLEA ESCAPED SCRATCH
ACT — CARLOS

The particulars on the back of this form should be completed.

Writing Your Own

The first purpose of a diary or log-book is to record events soon after they happen and so to aid one's memory or leave a record for others. Here are some of the last entries in the famous diary that Captain Scott kept on his tragic last expedition in the Antarctic—he and his companions are on the return journey from the South Pole.

Wednesday, March 21.—Got within 11 miles of depot Monday night;* had to lie up all yesterday in severe blizzard. To-day forlorn hope, Wilson and Bowers going to depot for fuel.

22 and 23—Blizzard bad as ever—Wilson and Bowers unable to start—to-morrow last chance—no fuel and only one or two (rations) of food left—must be near the end. Have decided it shall be natural —we shall march for the depot with or without our effects and die in our tracks.

(Thursday) March 29.—Since the 21st we have had a continuous gale from W.S.W. and S.W. We had fuel to make two cups of tea apiece and bare food for two days on the 20th. Every day we have been ready to start for our depot 11 miles away, but outside the door of the tent it remains a scene of whirling drift. I do not think we can hope for any better things now. We shall stick it out to the end, but we are getting weaker, of course, and the end cannot be far.

It seems a pity, but I do not think I can write more.

R. Scott.

Last entry. For God's sake look after our people.

*The 6oth camp from the Pole.

What reasons might one have for keeping a diary? In what ways is Giles Hopkins' diary more than a bare record of facts?

A diary is partly a record of events and partly a way of expressing your own impressions and feelings, and your reactions to events and people. Writing a diary regularly helps you to sort out your own ideas and to find a special kind of relief in expressing just what you feel—this is especially true if you decide to keep your diary strictly private.

Whether you decide to keep a private diary regularly from now on, or not, keep one for the next week at least, as a composition exercise. Try to make it as interesting as you can. If the events of the week are not in themselves very exciting, then introduce more personal comment and make the diary a record of your feelings and impressions. You may use a diary style of writing (not using "I" very often) if you wish.

Alternatively, write at least five days in an imaginary diary of a man or woman in some more exciting circumstances, perhaps exploring, or on a long, difficult journey, or on an exciting holiday. But if you choose to do this, you must pay careful attention to accurate detail, or it will seem unreal.

Things To Do

1. Letters and diaries are important forms of communication. Find out more about the postal and telephone services available in your area, for instance:

Where is the nearest post office?

How much do local calls from a phone-box cost?

How much (per minute) does it cost to make a call to Paris? How do you do this?

What does it cost to send the following to addresses in this country: letters; post-cards; printed papers; receipts; circulars; Christmas cards?

What is a greetings telegram? How much does it cost?

How can you find out the following by telephone: the time, the local weather forecast, a telephone number you cannot find in the directory?

What are the following: Registered Post, Express Letters, Recorded Delivery, airletters, the Business Reply Service?

You will probably find the *Post Office Guide* and the local *Telephone Directories* in your nearest public library and the post office.

2. Make up some other post-cards and telegrams (see *Exercise 5*), and discuss the art of getting as much as possible into the fewest words. Also, make some imaginary telephone calls. Imagine that you have to telephone a doctor about an accident, the fire-brigade giving details of a fire, or a friend to give him exact directions to reach your house (or the school) from some distant address. Discuss how to answer the telephone correctly. All these calls should be made in front of the class, so that the rest can criticise each one for any lack of clarity, politeness or accuracy.

3. Some pocket diaries give calendar information about feasts, holidays, anniversaries and official dates. Where would you look for this kind of information in the reference section of a library? Try to find out something about each of the following— what dates they fall on, what the terms mean or the days commemorate, whether they are public holidays, and so on:

Epiphany and Hogmanay; the Oxford and Cambridge University Terms (what they are called and how long they last); the beginning and end of partridge and other hunting seasons; Candlemas, Michaelmas and Martinmas; Quarter Days; the main Saints' Days; Plough Monday, Shrove Tuesday, Ash Wednesday, Maundy Thursday, Good Friday and Palm Sunday; Equinoxes and Solstices; Rogation Days and Ember Days; Lady Day; the Dog Days; Septuagesima, Sexagesima, etc.

Books To Read

Mayflower Boy by STANLEY YOUNG (Pickering and Inglis)
In this story, the author has added fiction to fact. Using the early diaries and records about the settlers and the Indians they had to deal with, he has bound the facts together with an exciting tale of a lad who grows up with the colony.

Scott's Last Expedition (from the Personal Journals of Capt. R. F. Scott) (Murray; Tandem)
The story of Scott's last journey to the South Pole, in close rivalry with Amundsen's Norwegian expedition, remains (as his son, Peter Scott, reminds us) "as timeless as the human spirit". Told in the words of his own diary, it is indeed exciting and inspiring.

The Long Winter by LAURA INGALLS WILDER (Lutterworth; Penguin)
This is the story of a family of American settlers, the Ingalls, during one harsh and cruel winter. They move from their farming claim land into the town, but even here it seems that they will run out of food, and only the perseverance and guidance of their mother brings the Ingalls children through.

The Golden Ocean by PATRICK O'BRIAN (Macmillan; Penguin)
In 1740 "H.M.S. Centurion" sailed round the world searching for Spanish treasure. Peter Palafox, a young Irish midshipman, accompanies Anson on that epic journey of heroism and endurance.

Son of Columbus by HANS BAUMANN (O.U.P.)
Columbus' son, Fernan, accompanies him on his fourth voyage of discovery to the West Indies. Storms, shipwreck, mutiny and hostile Indians make this an exciting voyage, but Fernan also makes friends with a Red Indian boy.

This story is set in the snowy wastes of the far north of America. Carcajou is another name for the wolverine, a member of the weasel family, and a beast feared and hated by all other wild animals.

CHAPTER EIGHT

Snow

The storm had broken after days of merciless driving. A cold sun shot its rays feebly across the snow-locked landscape. The whole world was in the grip of a glittering white silence. The snow was deeper than the oldest spruce had ever known, and the cold was greater. Trees popped and snapped under the strain, and no living thing ventured out. White famine had come to the high country. Death faced the dwellers of the vast silence.

The valley of the Unaweep saw no life that day. Towards evening a great horned owl beat along the ridges and fanned close to the snow-laden timber. His round, hard eyes stared down and to the side, and his beak clicked. He was used to stretches of starvation but not to weeks of it. Patiently he beat along the tireless pinyons. He was willing to strike at anything that lived.

Carcajou stepped out of a strip of spruce timber and peered into the dazzling world. He was truly hungry for the first time in many months. The great owl banked steeply and swept towards the spot where Carcajou was sitting. Down through the snapping air the feathered hunter whistled. Carcajou sat up and snarled. He was ready to feast upon owl, though that fare was ordinarily marked off his food list.

The great owl saw his mistake and beat to a halt, then slid off steeply to the right. He would gladly have torn the hulking black hunter beneath him to shreds had he dared, for he hated Carcajou. These two roving killers were alike in their relentless pursuit of game and alike in the fury of their attack.

Carcajou moved back under cover. The sun was still too high for him to hunt. His eyes would not stand the glare. In a half hour he would have been snow blind. The great owl had been braving the glittering slopes because he was starving.

With a savage grunt the killer lay down and composed himself to await the coming of dusk. Never before had he felt the grip of a gnawing desire for food. He had been hungry many times, but he had not known what it was to face a completely empty cupboard such as the Unaweep had offered for the past week . . . .

Slowly the pale sun dipped behind a ragged rim and the air became more brittle. A blue silence began to creep up the canyon and to wrap the high peaks in chill dusk. Now Carcajou came out, sniffing the snapping air. He grunted and made an attempt to look into the clearing below. In summer that clearing would have been dotted with at least two or three feeding deer. Now it was a vast spread of silent white.

Carcajou walked out into the open, shaking the frost from his mane. He was in a fierce mood that boded ill for any creature small or large whom he met.

Above him the great owl was still beating desperately along the slope. He was paying the penalty of hunger. His sally into the bright sunlight had done a terrible thing to him. Behind his hard, glassy eyeballs there was a raging and shooting pain. He could not see distinctly as he had always done in the early twilight. Twice he crashed through the upper limbs of an Engelmann spruce that rose in his path of flight. Each time he cleared himself with a ripping of talons and a clicking of his stout beak.

Whirling and idling, he drifted close to the ground in order to see any moving object that might venture out of the spruce, and swinging along uncertainly with angry clicks and hisses. Suddenly he saw a moving form not ten feet below him. He could not make out what it was, but it seemed to have risen on its legs and to be looking up. With a whirl and a mighty stroke the great bird descended.

(from *Carcajou* by Rutherford Montgomery)

For Discussion

1. What does "The storm had broken" mean here? What other meaning could it have?
2. Were the wolverine and the horned owl normally enemies?
3. In what ways were they in fact alike?
4. What important mistake did the owl make because of his hunger? Did Carcajou make the same mistake? How did the owl suffer for his mistake?
5. What difference did the sunshine make as far as these animals were concerned?
6. The "pinyons" (or "piñons") are American nut-pine trees. In what sense can they be called "tireless"?
7. Examine the ways in which the opening paragraph emphasizes the cold, especially the way in which the storm, the sun, the silence, the spruce and death are treated as if they were living creatures.
8. How does the passage suggest that it became even colder at dusk?
9. Discuss the meaning and effectiveness of these phrases:

   (the owl) fanned close   a ragged rim
   the snapping air   a blue silence
   (the owl) slid off steeply   a ripping of talons

10. Do you sympathize with either, or both, of these creatures? Is there any point in feeling sorry for wild animals that are killed off in winter? Why should people take time and trouble to put out food and unfrozen water for birds, or other wild creatures, in severe cold weather?

For Written Answers

1. What moving form did the owl see below in the twilight?
2. Write as full a description of the wolverine as you can from the evidence in this passage.
3. How long can a wolverine apparently exist without food, before becoming desperately hungry?
4. Write as full a description of the horned owl as you can.
5. How long can a horned owl exist without food?

Snow

No break of wind,
No gleam of sun —
Still the white snow
Whirls softly down —
Twig and bough
And blade and thorn
All in an icy
Quiet, forlorn.

Whispering, rustling,
Through the air,
On sill and stone,
Roof — everywhere,
It heaps its powdery
Crystal flakes;
Of every tree
A mountain makes;
Till pale and faint
At shut of day,
Stoops from the west
One wintry ray.
And, feathered in fire,
Where ghosts the moon,
A Robin shrills
His lonely tune.

WALTER DE LA MARE

Discussing the Poem

1. How does the poet emphasize that the snow covers *everything?* How can the snow be said to make a "mountain" of every tree?
2. What is the contrast between the description in the first sixteen lines of the poem, and that in the last eight? Does the robin make the scene seem more friendly and full of life?
3. Discuss the sense in which snow can be said to "whisper" or "rustle", in which "one wintry ray . . . stoops from the west", a robin is "feathered in fire", and the moon "ghosts".

Method Exercises

Examine these adjectives, taken from the passage.

A *cold* sun shot its rays feebly.
The snow was *deeper.*
Than the *oldest* spruce had ever known.
The cold was *greater.*
The air became *more brittle.*

Why do two of them end in -er and one in -est? How could we use these variations on the basic adjectives?

cold — colder — coldest
deep — deeper — deepest
old — older — oldest
great — greater — greatest
brittle — more brittle — most brittle

In each case, the first form is called the POSITIVE form of the adjective, the second the COMPARATIVE and the third the SUPERLATIVE. Can you explain these names? Comparatives are used when comparing *two* people, things, etc. The superlative is used for picking out the most extreme of three or more:

e.g. Tonight it is *cold*, but yesterday it was *colder* and last
Thursday was the *coldest* night of the winter so far.

With a few exceptions, most short adjectives add -er and -est to form the comparative and superlative, but whenever these would be clumsy to pronounce, we can use the separate words *more* and *most* instead.

Exercise 1. (a) Write out the positive, comparative and superlative of these adjectives:

    tall   sad   beautiful   late   bad
    large   grimy   hopeless   good   rugged

(b) Decide which form of the adjective is correct in the following sentences, and rewrite each sentence using it:

i. This must be the (lonely, lonelier, loneliest) lighthouse of all on that coast.

ii. The (handsome, handsomer, handsomest) of the two brothers was home on leave.

iii. I earned (few, fewer, fewest) penalties than all the other competitors.

iv. Indeed I had the (promising, more promising, most promising) round of all.

v. The (much, more, most) money you have, the (big, bigger, biggest) your contribution should be.

vi. Who is the (heavy, heavier, heaviest), Pat or Joan?

vii. Has Pat, Joan or Vi the (long, longer, longest) hair?

viii. That is a (clever, cleverer, cleverest) way to make a toboggan, but I know a(n) (ingenious, more ingenious, most ingenious) one than that.

Exercise 2. (a) The passage included some vivid, unusual and interesting nouns, verbs, adjectives and adverbs. Consider the following examples; what makes the words in italics effective? Can you find other, similar examples in the passage?

A cold sun *shot* its rays *feebly* across the *snowlocked* landscape.

Trees *popped* and *snapped* under the strain.

White famine had come to the high country.

A great horned owl *beat along* the ridges and *fanned* close to the *snow-laden* timber.

Down through the *snapping* air the *feathered hunter whistled*.

Slowly the pale sun *dipped* behind a *ragged rim* and the air became *more brittle*.

Which of the words in italics are nouns, which adjectives, which verbs and which adverbs?

(b) Rewrite the following sentences using more vivid nouns, adjectives, verbs and adverbs wherever you can. Introduce other words to expand them into much more interestingly written sentences.

   i. Snow fell on everything.
  ii. The car went up the hill.
 iii. The car slipped dangerously on the ice.
 iv. Snow made the birds hungry.
   v. Icicles were on the twigs and they caught the sunlight.
 vi. The wolf ate its prey hungrily.
 vii. Floodwater fell over the waterfall.
viii. Floodwater surrounded the cottages.
 ix. The sun shone through the trees.
  x. The glider flew up and down in the warm air.

Exercise 3. In English a group of words can often do the work of a single word. Such a group of words is called a PHRASE if it has no verb, and a CLAUSE if it includes a verb of its own. In the passage from *Carcajou*, we have examples of many phrases doing the work of adverbs—*adverb phrases* telling us how, when, where or why something happens.

> The storm had broken *after days of merciless driving*. (When had it broken?)
> A cold sun shot its rays feebly *across the snowlocked landscape*. (Where did it shoot its rays?)
> Trees popped and snapped *under the strain*. (How, or why, did they pop and snap?)

Here is an example of a "why" clause:

> The great owl had been braving the glittering slopes *because he was starving*. (Why had he been braving the slopes?)

What is the verb in the clause?

(a) In the following four sentences, adapted from the passage, the five adverb phrases have been put in italics. State what question each answers (as in the examples above), and choose a single adverb that might have been used instead of each phrase, from this list: later, downwards, there, alongside, angrily.

    i. White famine had come *to the high country*.

    ii. *Towards evening* a great horned owl beat *along the ridges*.

    iii. *Down through the snapping air* the feathered hunter whistled.

    iv. *With a savage grunt* the killer lay down.

(b) In the remaining five sentences, you have to pick out one adverb phrase from each, and write these out, stating what question each answers, as in the examples on page 107.

    v. In half an hour he would have been snow blind.

    vi. These two roving killers were alike in their relentless pursuit of game.

    vii. Slowly the pale sun dipped behind a ragged rim.

    viii. A blue silence began to creep up the canyon.

    ix. That clearing would have been dotted with at least two or three deer.

Exercise 4. Expand the following into fuller, more interesting sentences by substituting adverb phrases (or clauses) for the single adverbs printed in italics. You may rearrange the order of the sentence if necessary.

    e.g. The snow fell *thickly*.

        The snow fell in a curtain of clinging, woolly flakes.

(a) *Afterwards* the garden was knee-deep in snow.

(b) We played *there* with our sledge.

(c) We dragged our sledges *uphill*.

(d) We swept swiftly *down*.

(e) The sledges sped *smoothly* over the ice.

(f) We *then* felt hungry and trudged *wearily* home.

(g) The hungry wolf turned *angrily* on the hunters.

(h) One of the men was *very quietly* creeping up with a net.

(i) *Very swiftly* he threw the net over the beast.

(j) The wolf was *therefore* caught.

Exercise 5. As we saw in Chapter 7, synonyms are words of similar meaning, but there is often a slight difference in meaning between them, so that only one may be correct in a particular sentence:

e.g. The door was quite (surely, securely) fastened.
"Securely" is the correct word.

Rewrite the following sentences, using (and underlining) the correct word.

(a) The young man was utterly (untrue, untruthful) in all he said to the policeman.

(b) The walls were one metre (wide, thick) but there were (wide, thick) gaps in them for doors and windows.

(c) Before the beginning of the race, each (competitor, rival) was given a number to wear.

(d) The party set out to (explore, reconnoitre) the unmapped areas of the Upper Amazon.

(e) There was a (mutiny, rebellion) among the troops sent to deal with the (mutiny, rebellion) against the island's governor.

(f) This (frail, fragile) old woman inspired a (revolution, revolt) in the treatment of prisoners.

(g) His answer was (hasty, rapid) and ill-considered.

(h) They enforced the rules (strictly, severely) and punished offenders (strictly, severely).

(i) This (famous, notorious) police chief successfully tackled the (famous, notorious) criminal gangs in the city.

(j) Your stop-watch may be working (correctly, accurately) but it is not sufficiently (correct, accurate) for timing this experiment.

Writing Your Own

Prepare for this composition by making full notes. Make a survey of the winter scene. Look at the trees, bushes and grass. Does winter sunshine seem different from summer sunshine? Look at the frost and ice; pick up a sheet of ice one morning and look through it, feel it, break it. Study the birds and other animal life in winter. If you have the opportunity, go out into snow while it is falling. Notice how it falls and how it lies. Is snow always white? Does it always lie evenly over every part of the landscape? Take some snow and press it; watch it melt; if you can, examine snow-flakes under a microscope or magnifying glass.

Make a list of suitable adjectives, verbs or phrases (look again at Exercise 2). Explore possible comparisons to describe what you see, hear, smell, taste and feel on a winter's day (or night).

Write a description of any typical winter scene, trying to make it as vivid and exciting as is the description from *Carcajou*. Here are a few suggestions:

> A park in winter, bleak and cold.
> A tobogganing scene.
> A skating scene.
> Your garden as snow falls.
> Any snow scene, in town or country.
> Animal habits in winter.

Things To Do

1. As a short composition, give full and clear instructions for *one* of the following:
   (a) Building a simple toboggan.
   (b) Learning to ice-skate.
   (c) Playing ice-hockey.
   (d) Helping birds and other wild creatures in very severe weather.
   (e) Making a snowman.

Pay particular attention to working out the correct order for the instructions; and make your style simple and direct. You are not telling a story, only giving instructions.

2. Write an animal story, or perhaps one continuing the struggle between Carcajou and the owl, set in winter, for the next issue of the class magazine.

Alternatively write a winter poem. Study Walter de la Mare's *Snow* before you begin, and, without necessarily trying to make your poem rhyme, write as vividly and directly as you can.

3. Prepare a talk on some aspect of winter: for instance, any of the winter sports and pastimes (including ski-jumping, ice-yachting, figure-skating, bob-sleighing, etc.), the weather in winter (difference between frost, snow, sleet, hail, rain and dew, or the cause of winter fogs), animals or plant life in winter, winter flowers, both wild and cultivated, precautions against snow and ice on roads or railways, machines such as snow-ploughs, motor sledges, snow track-vehicles, ice-breakers, or winter in various other countries, etc.

Books To Read

Carcajou by RUTHERFORD MONTGOMERY (Longmans; Penguin)
The wolverine Carcajou is full of vengeance against a brave, simple Indian who is struggling to keep his friend, "Mister Jim", a lumbering, good-humoured grizzly bear.
Winter Holiday by ARTHUR RANSOME (Cape; Penguin)
This is one of Arthur Ransome's famous series of books set in mid-winter in the Lake District, and it includes the rescue of a crag-fast sheep in the snow as well as an exciting race to the "north pole" on an ice-yacht across the frozen lake.
Avalanche by ANNA RUTGERS VAN DER LOEFF (translated by Dora Round) (Brockhampton; Penguin)
Werner and his schoolmaster father save the lives of Paolo and other Italian orphans from the Pestalozzi Village who are on holiday in Werner's village in the Swiss Alps. Then the avalanche strikes, and Werner's father is believed killed. Werner and Paolo form a strong friendship which is to last long after Werner's parents are in fact found alive after all.
The Wolves of Willoughby Chase by JOAN AIKEN (Cape; Penguin)
Set in an imaginary past, when wolves ravaged the frozen North of 19th-century England, this is a wild, fantastic story about two exceptional girls, Sylvia and Bonnie, and a grim governess. The hero of this story, Simon, returns in *Black Hearts in Battersea*, the next in a series of funny, exciting fantasies by this popular author.

This story is set in a working-class neighbourhood of an industrial town where the barber's shop is run as a part-time occupation by Rag Bob, the local rag-and-bone merchant, and his wife, Alice.

CHAPTER NINE

The Shop Round The Corner

It was to his shop I went one Friday afternoon to have my hair cut. My dad had been nagging me that much about it, until he got fed up and said he wouldn't give me my Friday's sixpence until it had been cut. I hated the idea of having a haircut because, apart from the ordeal of plucking and itching and keeping still, there was always something warm and matey about having long thick hair covering your neck and hanging like a fringe over your jersey collar.

There was no getting out of it, except to go without spending money, so at half-past four I went into Rag Bob's.

The saloon, as it was called, was the front room of an ordinary two-up and two-down cottage. It had no fancy equipment, and the stone floor was white from rubbing stone, and your clogs made a nice clack when walking over it. The haircutting and shaving seats were old-fashioned chairs with no sliding backs. The boys' chair was a rocking chair with the rockers sawn off. The hot water came from a big iron kettle on the hob. The gaslight was on all the time because of the big spinning-mill just across the narrow street, from which a cool dark shadow spread over the cottages on sunny days. In fact, you could feel the floor vibrating from the machinery across the way as you sat on your chair. All in all, it was a very homely barber-shop . . . .

It was six o'clock when Bob put me up on the high chair, and fastened the sheet round my neck, picked up the heavy, old-fashioned clippers and began to press and drive them up the back of my head. He was a very mannerly chap, and if you hadn't been for a haircut for six months, which I hadn't, he would never make any comment about it. I was looking through the mirror, watching Alice lather this chap from the tannery who had a big Adam's apple.

The chap gave a sour grunt. "Watch what you're doing," he said.

"I'm watching what I'm doing," said Alice.

"Then what do you keep shovin' it up my nose for?"

"Shovin' what up your nose?" said Alice.

"Lather," he said. "You keep shovin' lather up me nose."

"Don't be so soft," said Alice. "Anyway, you're not too big to have a bit of soap up your nose."

At this Bob turned to Alice. "Now, that's enough, Alice," he said quietly.

"Do you mind keeping your big nose out of this?" said Alice to Bob.

"My wife wouldn't have to talk to me like that," said the man with the Adam's apple.

At once I felt Bob's grip tighten on the top of my head.

"I never knew you had a wife," said Alice.

"I haven't," said the chap in the chair. "I mean, if I 'ad one."

"You needn't worry about that," said Alice, "you never will have one so long as you've got an Adam's apple like that. It sticks out like Blackpool Tower."

"*Alice!* " hissed Bob. "Shut up!" I could feel those fingers almost crushing my head in.

"I'm not standing for it," said the chap in the chair, trying to rise. Alice just forced his head back and started rubbing all the thick, lathery soap all over his nose and eyes.

The chap shouted and squirmed, and then Bob let go of me and grabbed at Alice. But she swung free of him. "You men are all alike," she yelled out, "each rotten miserable one of you thinks he's a lord of creation." Then she snatched the shaving mug she had been using, and flung the hot, soapy water all over Bob. He let out a terrible roar. Alice flew to the door, jumping over the clogged feet of the customers. Then she slammed it after her. Bob flung down the clippers, picked up a razor, and chased after her. Away up the street I could hear him howling as he ran after her.

(from *The Haircut*, a short story in *The Goalkeeper's Revenge*
by Bill Naughton)

For Discussion

1. Describe a "two-up and two-down" cottage.
2. What are "sliding backs" on barbers' chairs and what are they for?
3. What would "old-fashioned clippers" be like? What else seems old-fashioned about this barber's?
4. In what ways does this passage illustrate that Bob "was a very mannerly chap"?
5. What were Alice's feelings about men in general and Bob in particular? Was she justified, do you think?
6. What indications are there in the passage that the story is set in the North of England?
7. Do you know anyone who still wears clogs in this country? Where were they once worn very commonly in the British Isles? What foreign country are they associated with?
8. What were the boy's various reasons for putting off his haircut? Do you agree with any or all of them? Do you like long hair-styles for men?
9. Did either Bob or Alice seem to believe that the customer is always right? Is this a good motto for a shopkeeper?
10. How do you think this story ended? After you have discussed possible endings, someone should borrow a copy of the book from a library and read the whole story to the class.

115

1. Did Bob and Alice have gas or electricity? How did they heat the shaving water?
2. What effects did the mill have on the barber-shop?
3. How did Alice and Bob divide the work in the shop?
4. How did Bob show his annoyance at first?
5. What does "My wife wouldn't have to talk to me like that" mean?

Method Exercises

Just as phrases can do the work of a single adverb, and describe a verb, so phrases can do the work of an adjective, and describe a noun. In the passage we read of:

chairs *with no sliding backs,*

the big spinning mill *just across the narrow street.*

The phrases in italics describe the chairs and the mill, and distinguish them from other chairs and other mills.

What is described by the ADJECTIVE PHRASES in italics in each of the following sentences, adapted from the passage?

The boys' chair was a rocking chair *with the rockers sawn off.*

The floor vibrated from the machinery *across the way.*

He would never make any comment *about it.*

Alice lathered this chap *from the tannery.*

So said the man *with the Adam's apple.*

The chap *in the chair* tried to rise.

Alice jumped over the clogged feet *of the customers.*

In most of these cases it would be difficult to think of a single adjective that could do exactly the same work as the adjective phrase. In the following, however, the phrase and the adjective mean the same.

He was a man *of great strength.*

He was a *strong* man.

Exercise 1. Rewrite the following sentences, replacing the adjective phrases in italics by single adjectives of much the same meaning:

(a) Those hills *in the distance* are the Cotswolds.
(b) We found we had hired a horse *with a limp*.
(c) They found a pram *without any wheels*.
(d) They brought the climber *with the injury* down the mountain.
(e) We have a cottage *in the country*.
(f) The tunnel *under the ground* caved in during the floods.
(g) Joan stayed in the hotel *beside the lake*.
(h) Bill was the driver *of a bus*.
(i) Her answer was quite *out of the ordinary*.
(j) His was the only barber's shop *in that area*.

Exercise 2. Rewrite the following, replacing the adjectives in italics by adjective phrases of similar meaning.

(a) The *hill-top* castle was never captured.
(b) The *red-haired* girl was the one who fell.
(c) *Blond* film-stars were very popular at that time.
(d) In such lonely country, a *roadside* inn draws a lot of business.
(e) *Farm* workers were underpaid.
(f) All the *nearby* houses were being sold.
(g) Some *Japanese* shrubs grew by the stream.
(h) The *bearded* singer then took the guitar and sang.
(i) As a Member of Parliament, he needed a *town* flat as well as a *country* house.

Exercise 3. Each of the following *adverb phrases*, printed in italics in these sentences, could be replaced by one of the adverbs in this list:

> dully, duly; luxuriantly, luxuriously;
> crudely, rudely; respectfully;
> shyly, slyly; successively, successfully;
> truly, truthfully; warily, wearily.

Use a dictionary to check the meaning of any you do not know and rewrite the sentences using the single adverb in place of the phrase.

(a) They trudged home *in a tired way.*

(b) He gave his answers *with complete honesty.*

(c) The hut was built *with rough, unfinished materials.*

(d) The speaker talked *in a dull way* of his experiences.

(e) She blushed and answered *in a timid voice.*

(f) They proceeded *with great caution* over the snake-infested rocks.

(g) He was *without any doubt* a born violinist.

(h) The young men pushed past the waiting queue *in an impolite manner.*

(i) We raised our hats *to show our deference.*

(j) They were smiling *in a cunning and mischievous way.*

(k) The King was crowned *in the proper way and at the proper time.*

(l) The operation was completed *with considerable success.*

(m) The three men each bowled *one after another.*

(n) The creeper had grown *in great profusion,* and covered the whole wall.

(o) The room was furnished *in luxury and comfort.*

Exercise 4. To give the feeling of a northern town, the conversation in the passage is written and spelt to suggest the northern accent of the speakers. People in all regions of Britain have their own accents and dialects: their own ways of pronouncing words and their own variations of standard English grammar. In the passage, the man with the Adam's apple says:

"You keep shovin' lather up me nose."

What words here would have to be changed to make this standard English?

In the following exercise, there is one correction to be made in each sentence to change it into correct, standard English. Rewrite them correctly:

e.g. I had been there ten minutes when I see Joan in the distance.

Answer: I had been there ten minutes when I <u>saw</u> Joan in the distance.

(a) He has bought hisself a motorcycle.
(b) I have forgotten all me fishing tackle.
(c) I been waiting here an hour or more.
(d) I found I had done the homework wrong.
(e) After tea they gave theirselves a treat and went down to the amusement arcade.
(f) Did you collect them parcels for me?
(g) I ran faster than I ever done before in my life.
(h) We managed to get fifty pence off of him for the charity.
(i) Bill, George, Ted and me all went to report the loss at the police station.
(j) My friends and I were given a form and was told to fill it in.

Exercise 5. A very large department store lists the following departments at the entrance:

antiques	glassware	off licence
confectionery	haberdashery	optical
crockery	hosiery	pharmacy
cutlery	household linen	poultry
delicatessen	ironmongery	soft furnishing
electrical	jewelry	sportswear
estate agency	millinery	stationery
garden equipment	monumental masonry	travel agency
		valet service

Which of these departments would you go to for the following?

sweets	a duck
a poultice	rye bread
an iron	a stoneware casserole
some cup-hooks	curtain material
carbon paper	a Victorian gramophone
a pair of ear-rings	a pair of stockings
a lady's hat	to have a suit cleaned
a set of buttons	a pair of spectacles
to rent a country cottage	a set of pillow-cases
for information about	ski-boots
visiting country houses	a carving knife
a headstone for a grave	a bottle of wine
a decanter	a pruning knife

Writing Your Own

Choose a shop in your area that you know well, and one that has a distinctive air about it. It would be best to select a small, personal business run by a shopkeeper with a strong personality of his own which is imprinted on his shop. Make notes before you begin to describe the shop or its owner.

First, the shop: what does it sell? Where is it? What impression does it give from outside? Inside, has it a special smell? Are there particular sounds associated with it? What is the first impression as you enter? How is this built up as you look around more closely?

Secondly, the shopkeeper or assistant: make notes about his or her appearance, the voice, mannerisms, kind of clothes, the jokes he makes and generally how he treats the customers.

Thirdly, work out how the owner fits the shop. Is it an expression of his personality? Does he apparently enjoy running his shop? Is it a success, a friendly place where one is tempted to spend one's time and money? If so, try to show why this is so.

Now write your composition entitled:

THE SHOP ROUND THE CORNER

Things To Do

1. The class could make a survey of prices in local shops. First, agree on a list of *basic* shopping requirements for ordinary housekeeping, subdivided if it seems necessary (e.g. English butter and foreign butter). In each case, decide on a simple quantity (500g butter, 250g tea, 1 kilo gran. sugar, 1 kilo potatoes etc.). Then divide into groups to cover different shops or different areas, and different kinds of goods. When you visit the shop, note down the cheapest basic prices of the goods on your list; also take note of any concessions, such as trading stamps or free gifts, that the shop may be offering. Do *not* worry the assistants with a lot of questions. Back at school the information could be compiled and presented as a series of charts, something like the one begun in the illustration, with written notes to accompany them. Finally, draw some conclusions about where to go to buy most economically in your area; but take into account the expense of time and money in travelling! What other considerations should also be taken into account when deciding where you get the best value for money?

	Co-op. High St.	Brown's North Rd.	Supermarket High St.	Fairlie's Park Ave.
250g Danish Butter	25½p	25½p	25p	27p
1kg Gran. Sugar	25½p	25½p	25½p	26p
500g N.Z. Cheese	58p	60p	58p	61p
6 Standard Eggs	22p	22½p	22p	23p
500g Patna Rice	27½p	28p	27p	29p

2. Find out what the following mean or are:

an auction	a "job lot"
a lot	on sale or return
a Dutch auction	made to measure
a store detective	"off the peg"
a shop-walker	a "second"
(or floor-walker)	C.O.D.
a buyer	a cash refund
a sale	a credit note
a bargain basement	a cash register (or till)
a remnant	a cafeteria
a shop-soiled article	a bill
price maintenance	a receipt
discount	

3. The story of *The Haircut* should be a good subject for an impromptu play, whether you use the plot of the complete short story, or whether you use this opening situation only and develop the story along your own lines. Clearly there is room for interesting characterisation among the customers, and once each actor has firmly established the kind of person he is, there should be no need for a complete script: work the conversation out as the play goes on.

The Goalkeeper's Revenge by BILL NAUGHTON (Heinemann; Penguin)
This collection of short stories is for boys and is mainly about boys—boys fishing, boys fighting, boys playing football, boys in hospital or going for a job. And most of the stories are funny.

Silver Everything and *Many Mansions* by WINIFRED CAWLEY (O.U.P.)
Two down-to-earth stories about Tyneside in the 1920s, both centred on Jinnie, who clings firmly to her family pride, even when they have to take the corner shop in Stratford Street.

The Boy at the Window by E. W. HILDICK (Chatto and Windus)
David Case is confined to bed in a room over his mother's drapery store, and he becomes increasingly mystified by the suspicious behaviour of visitors to the sweet-shop opposite, and of the other shop-keepers in the road. With the help of the school-friends who regularly visit him (and some hindrance from their pet mouse, who takes up residence in the sick room!), David eventually solves this exciting mystery.

Me and My Million by CLIVE KING (Penguin)
If Elvis will trust this valuable picture, stolen from Kenwood House, to a kid brother who can't tell a 14 bus from a 41, things are bound to get complicated; and in this lively story (by the author of *Stig of the Dump*), set firmly in the heart of London, they certainly do.

Supplementary Exercises

Analysis Exercise 1

One way of setting out the subject and verb of a sentence is like this:

SUBJECT —————————VERB

The ship —————————returned

This can be expanded into a diagram to show the subject word, with any adjectives describing it, and the verb with any adverbs attached to it:

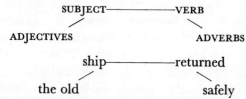

What sentence has been ANALYSED in this example? Notice that *the* and *a(n)* are treated as adjectives.

(a) Analyse the following simple statement sentences on this pattern:

   i. She succeeded.

  ii. She certainly did succeed.

 iii. The wobbly chair collapsed completely.

 iv. The faithful old dog slept soundly.

  v. The green bus did run yesterday.

 vi. He has been working today.

 vii. The steam pump was running well.

viii. His mother had been seriously worried.

 ix. Then the last bewildered onlookers dispersed.

  x. A fine, gleaming, old vintage car swept gracefully past.

(b) These diagrams, of course, cannot represent variations in word order. *Questions* are set out like statements. What question has been analysed here?

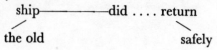

124

What *exclamation* is represented here?

pump————————was running
／ ＼
the steam   how well

Notice that "how" is part of the adverb.

Commands normally have their subject, *you* "understood". What command is represented here?

(you)————————reply
＼
immediately

Analyse the following questions, exclamations or commands.

    i. Did she arrive safely?
   ii. Does the green bus run today?
  iii. How well he could paint!
  iv. How well could he paint?
    v. Keep left.
   vi. Are you coming now?
 vii. Come now.
viii. Has the chief guest arrived yet?
  ix. How brightly the sun shone there!
   x. Does she intend to go back today?

Analysis Exercise 2

This GRAPHIC ANALYSIS pattern can be further expanded to include *objects*, which are placed underneath the verb, with their adjectives below and to the left.

SUBJECT————————VERB
／ | ＼
ADJECTIVES   ADVERBS
OBJECT
／
ADJECTIVES

What sentence has been analysed here?

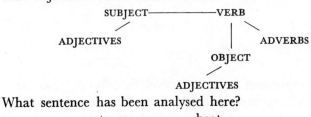

team————————beat
／ | ＼
the second   convincingly
team
／
the first

(a) Analyse the following statements in this way:

    i. We fastened the door.

   ii. This horse has won many races.

  iii. Our neighbours have bought a new car.

   iv. They have been cleaning it today.

    v. I have just heard the news.

   vi. The men are rebuilding the church.

  vii. I have been learning French.

viii. Young apprentices must learn the safety regulations first.

   ix. Once a young girl was visiting her grandmother.

    x. Experienced sailors rapidly lowered the dinghy.

(b) When questions, exclamations and commands have objects they are again a little more complicated.

What question has been analysed in this example?

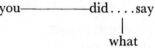

Notice that question words like *what, whose, which, who, whom* are either pronouns or adjectives; words like *when, where, how, why* will be adverbs.

What exclamation has been analysed here?

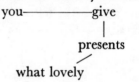

Here, the word *what* is an adjective, describing "presents".
  Thirdly, what command has been analysed in this example?

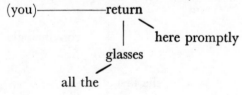

Analyse each of the following in the appropriate way:

    i. Did you speak?

   ii. Did you say something?

  iii. What did you say?

  iv. What lovely food you provide!

   v. Do you spend a lot?

  vi. Open the door quickly.

 vii. Which bus leaves first?

viii. Who has been eating all the cake?

  ix. Return the plates there.

   x. What a load you have there!

Analysis Exercise 3

In graphic analysis, *adverb phrases* can be shown in the same position as adverbs, as in this example:

He sold his bicycle the other day

```
he————————sold
                   ╲
              |       the other day
           bicycle
              ╱
          his
```

Notice that we treat the adverb phrase *as a unit*, and do not split off the adjectives, and also that the analysis would be exactly the same for the sentence:

The other day he sold his bicycle.

Analyse the following sentences, some of which contain adverb phrases.

(a) On the way he met a tramp.

(b) The tramp disappeared round the corner.

(c) She returned last night.

(d) He met her after the party.

(e) They ascended the hill in the rain.

(f) The poisoned arrow narrowly missed its mark.

(g) Her last dance impressed the audience very much.

(h) Wild tribesmen attacked the hill fortress.

(i) Boats can only leave the harbour with difficulty.

(j) On windy days boats can only leave with difficulty.

Analysis Exercise 4

Adjective phrases do the work of adjectives, and can therefore be shown in graphic analysis wherever there is a place for adjectives, as in this example:

That house down the hill collapsed the other day.

house————collapsed
/ \
that, down the hill   the other day

Notice that the sentence:

The other day that house down the hill collapsed.

would be analysed in exactly the same way; but the sentence:

The other day that house collapsed down the hill.

would have to show *two* adverb phrases, and no adjective phrase. Explain this.

Analyse the following sentences, most of which include adverb or adjective phrases, or both.

(a) He often climbed the tree with the pink blossom.
(b) He often climbed trees with his rope ladder.
(c) A ticket to the West Indies costs a lot.
(d) The thieves stole a lorry full of bicycles.
(e) After a good breakfast, the party left the hostel.
(f) Deep in thought, James strolled down the lane.
(g) The vicar started a special service for animal lovers.
(h) Did you see any deer in the forest?
(i) The deer in the forest ate the bark on the trees.
(j) Watch those deer in the clearing.

Revision Exercise 1

All the following words contain *silent letters*. Rearrange them in seven groups of six words, so that each group represents one silent letter. For example,

knapsack, knee, knell, knob, penknife, knuckle

all have a silent –k–.

knack	stalk	wreck	psalm	gnat
guess	yolk	knave	rhapsody	guilt
aghast	gnome	pneumonia	knock	wren
kneel	rhubarb	pseudonym	psychic	talk
gnu	build	knowledge	ghost	wriggle
walk	knit	rheumatism	plague	wreath
disguise	gnaw	rhododendron	wrinkle	psalter
guide	wrist	psychology	folk	caulk
gnarled	gnash			

Revision Exercise 2

(a) One way of representing contracted (or shortened) words is with an apostrophe to represent an omitted letter or letters. Write the contracted forms of the following word or words in each case:

    i. of the clock   v. he has   viii. forecastle

    ii. will not   vi. you are   ix. they will

    iii. over   vii. shall not   x. madam.

    iv. it would

Write the full forms of the following contractions which have apostrophes:

    xi. 'em   xv. we'll   xviii. penn'orth

    xii. they're   xvi. we'd   xix. sou'wester

    xiii. ain't   xvii. 'tis   xx. e'er.

    xiv. it's

(b) Another kind of contraction is the abbreviation, using full stops and initial letters or some of the letters in the full word. Write the abbreviations for each of these:

    i. etcetera   v. assistant   viii. limited

    ii. nota bene   vi. baronet   ix. for example

    iii. anno domini   vii. Bedfordshire   x. Lieutenant-

    iv. ante meridian   Colonel.

Write out the full forms of the following abbreviations:

    xi. i.e.   xv. Oxon.   xviii. O.H.M.S.

    xii. p.m.   xvi. M.C.C.   xix. kg

    xiii. P.M.   xvii. q.v.   xx. A.A.

    xiv. recd

Revision Exercise 3

The other important use of the apostrophe is for the possessive
—to show the owner of some thing or quality. Rewrite the
following in a form using an apostrophe, for example:

the death of Caesar—Caesar's death
hats for ladies—ladies' hats

(a) a vest for a boy
(b) a playground for boys
(c) the favourite of the duke
(d) pearls owned by a duchess
(e) the door of the store
(f) the door of the stores

(g) the tail of the ass
(h) the policy of those shops
(i) the top-deck of the bus
(j) the snow of last year
(k) rainfall over three days
(l) lives of other men.

Revision Exercise 4

The following sentences use made-up words, in a similar way
to those on page 28. One or two of the verbs, nouns, pronouns,
adjectives or adverbs in each are in italics. State first whether
this is a verb, noun etc.; then, if it is a verb, say whether it is
past, present or future tense; if it is a noun or pronoun, say
whether it is subject or object; if it is an adjective or adverb,
say what noun or verb it describes.
For example:

Will some fids *be plinking wocks* here? (2)
Will be plinking—verb, future tense
wocks—noun (plural), object.

(a) All *fids* can plink.
(b) Fids plink *wocks* and *swisps*. (2)
(c) Most fids *plink bannily*. (2)
(d) They are then *banny* fids.
(e) Fids *are* always *plinking*.
(f) A fid *was plinking* a wock bannily to show a little fid.
(g) How bannily *it plinked*! (2)
(h) Little fids are called *fidlings*.
(i) This fidling *plinked* yesterday.
(j) Was its first *plink* a good one?
(k) *Has* this *fidling plinked* bannily? (2)

Revision Exercise 5

Rewrite the following short story in seven paragraphs (remembering that a new paragraph is required for each new speaker in a conversation), inserting all the necessary punctuation, including capital letters.

What did i hit then said mr reed to himself as he pulled up on a country lane one night i had better have a look he found that his car had run over a hare in the road another car drew up behind him and the driver got out whats the trouble asked the stranger i hit a hare and i think ive killed it replied mr reed the stranger looked at the motionless animal went back to his car and returned with a small bottle he poured some of the liquid over the hare which immediately jumped up and ran off my goodness what miracle-working liquid was that asked the astonished mr reed oh nothing special replied the stranger only hair restorer

Revision Exercise 6

(a) Change all the *subject* words of the following sentences from singular to plural, making any other *necessary* changes.
  i. He knows me well.
  ii. After a long spell in hospital, the last casualty from the air crash was discharged fit and well.
  iii. Out of the wood steals a prowling wolf.
  iv. Who am I to tell him the truth?
  v. My aunt's brother-in-law is hardly a close relative of mine.

(b) Change all the *object* words of the following sentences into the plural, again with any necessary changes.
  i. He has seen me often enough.
  ii. The manager paid his employee well.
  iii. The well-known naturalist is bringing a hippopotamus back to the London Zoo.
  iv. The chauffeur cleaned his lordship's Rolls-Royce himself.
  v. He should not kill the goose that lays the golden egg.
     (*Two objects*)

131

Seven boys and girls, their ages ranging from nine to fifteen, obtain permission to convert a disused hall into their own "Blue Door Theatre" They are about to put on their first concert . . . .

CHAPTER TEN

First Night

On the walk to the theatre they discussed how they felt. Maddy said she felt just ordinary, but this was only bravado, for she was shivering violently, though the evening was anything but cold. Lyn said she felt excited and "wound up inside". To herself she was pretending that it was her first "first night" on a West End stage. Sandra, when asked, could only reply, "I feel worried," and did not disclose her physical feelings. The boys said they felt "a bit het up," and judging from the pinkness of Bulldog's complexion he suffered most.

Outside the theatre they looked up at the sign.

"Tons of people will be seeing this for the first time to-night," remarked Sandra. "I wonder what they'll say?"

Their footsteps echoed as they walked up the side of the hall, that had an expectant, waiting look, with the chairs facing the drawn curtains. They went into the dressing-room, neat and tidy at the moment.

"How different it will look at ten o'clock to-night," Lyn said.

"But not *too* different," warned Sandra, "or you'll hear about it. Now start getting dressed, and this is the only time you'll be able to dawdle to-night."

They got themselves into their Spanish clothes and Sandra made them up. Maddy screwed up her face.

"It feels all stiff and cracky," she grumbled.

"You look sweet. Now go and sit quietly somewhere."

Maddy found a chair and sat down on it. Her stomach seemed to be making a violent effort to escape. When Bulldog was ready he went out on to the stage and tested the curtains, then arranged the properties—low benches and a barrel supposed to contain wine. Jeremy, white underneath his tan make-up came across to the piano, which stood on the opposite side of the stage covered by the curtains, and arranged his music and tuned his violin. The familiar feel of it under his chin restored his confidence. Lyn was gazing at her face in the mirror with a haunted look in her eyes; she now knew what stage fright was. Sandra, her hands clasped under her chin, was pacing up and down like a caged lion. Although none of the audience had arrived they spoke in whispers . . . .

The hands of the clock pointed to two minutes to seven.

"If you forget your exact words, say something that means the same thing, but above all *act*," urged Lyn.

"We go on in one minute!"

Maddy clutched hold of Jeremy's hand. "I can't!" she whispered. "I shall be sick!"

Jeremy gulped and squeezed her hand reassuringly. "I feel like that too, Maddy, but we'll be all right after the first few minutes." . . . .

Mr. Fayne said, "Seven o'clock." Vicky squeaked. "My castanets!" and dived back into the dressing-room for them.

The boys lined themselves up on the front of the stage for the opening chorus. Jeremy played the first few bars and someone rattled a tambourine. Instantly the hall was in darkness. The boys stepped in front of the curtain. Vicky rattled the tambourine, and on went the stage lights.

(from *The Swish of the Curtain* by Pamela Brown)

For Discussion

1. What can we deduce about the first item in their concert from the evidence about it here?
2. What do you think were Bulldog's chief responsibilities? What would his title be in a larger stage company?
3. Why do actors wear "make-up"?
4. Explain the terms:

   bravado   properties
   "first night"   stage fright
   a West End stage   castanets

5. Discuss the different ways in which Maddy, Bulldog, Jeremy, Lyn, Sandra and Vicky showed their nervousness. Are there any other common signs of nervous tension?
6. What did the various members of the company do to help restore their confidence or cover up their nervousness? Can you think of other suggestions for overcoming nerves or stage fright?
7. Try to explain and expand Lyn's final advice to them.
8. Is it likely that they were "all right after the first few minutes"? If so, why?
9. If acting in public is so nerve-racking, what is so attractive about it?
10. What qualities make a good actor? Are these any different for an actor in a television or a film studio?

For Written Answers

1. What time was the concert due to begin?
2. Why did Lyn have a haunted look?
3. Take each of the six actors mentioned (Jeremy, Bulldog, Sandra, Lyn, Vicky and Maddy) and write at least a sentence about each one, using all the evidence you can find in the passage about their ages, ambitions, fears, interests, etc.

Method Exercises

We have learnt the difference between subject and object: it may be very important to know whether a policeman hurt a hooligan or the hooligan hurt the policeman! Frequently, however, a sentence will continue to say more about the subject, instead of introducing a different object, as in:

The hooligan eventually became a policeman.

Here the hooligan and the policeman are the same person.

This happens most commonly with the verb "to be" (is, are, was, were, am, have been, will be, etc.) which can never be followed by an object, because the sentence will always continue to speak about the same person thing or idea. In each of the following, we are talking about *one* person

The captain is the *centre-forward*.

The centre-forward became *captain*.

But this is not so in these two sentences:

The captain blamed the centre-forward.

The centre-forward disliked the captain.

In the first two examples, the words "centre-forward" and "captain" cannot be called objects; we therefore call them COMPLEMENTS, because they complete or *complement* (= add to) the subject.

Exercise 1. (a) Pick out the objects and complements from the following sentences. State what the verb is, in each case, and underline the object or complement word.

e.g. The last rose seemed a beautiful specimen.

"a beautiful *specimen*," complement of "seemed".

   i. She always grew beautiful roses.

  ii. The experiment seemed a disaster.

 iii. The experiment prevented a disaster.

 iv. We are amateur actors.

  v. We admire professional actors.

 vi. We hope to become professional actors.

 vii. Sir Alexander Fleming discovered penicillin.

viii. Sir Alexander Fleming was a famous scientist.

 ix. The doctor felt a fool.

  x. The doctor felt the lump in the boy's neck.

(b) Explain the following newspaper headlines, showing whether they are using complements or objects. Those marked with an asterisk * could have two meanings:

> e.g.* Explorer Returns Cannibal Chief.

This could mean that the explorer has returned from an expedition on which he was made a chief by some cannibals, in which case "chief" is complement of "returns". Alternatively, it means that he is sending a cannibal chief back to someone, somewhere ("chief" is then object of "returns").

   i. Mechanic Becomes Boss.
   ii. Mechanic Criticises Boss.
   iii. Thief Turned Detective.
   iv. Thief Turned Car Over.
   v.* Electricity Supplies the Answer.
   vi.* Post Delays Serious Matter.
   vii.* Bone Remains Only Evidence.
   viii.* Magazine Continues Weekly Supplement.

Exercise 2. (a) Instead of verbs with complements and verbs with objects, many sentences have verbs that require neither complement nor object. Rewrite the sentences in this exercise, underlining the verb (remember that it may be more than one word), and state whether it has an object or complement or neither. (Adverbs and adverb phrases, of course, can be added to *any* kind of verb.) Set answers out like this:

> e.g. i. James *was* a king. (subj.—verb—complement)
>   ii. James *used to write* books. (subj.—verb—object)
>   iii. James *ruled* for several years. (subj.—verb)

  i. Baden-Powell founded the Boy Scouts.
  ii. Baden-Powell himself became Chief Scout.
  iii. Baden-Powell died in 1941.
  iv. You ought to join a scout troop.
  v. You ought to be a scout.
  vi. On Thursday the weather changed.
  vii. The heat melted the tar on the roads.
  viii. The butter melted in the cupboard.
  ix. Smith will continue captain of the team.
  x. Smith will continue the same goal-scoring tactics.

(b) Complete the following with a suitable complement, object or adverb phrase, as indicated:

> e.g.   He returned . . . (adverb—how?)
> Answer: He returned on the last train.

   i. He returned . . . (adverb—when?)
   ii. He returned . . . (object—what?)
  iii. The jewels were . . . (complement—what?)
  iv. The jewels were . . . (adverb—where?)
   v. The only occupant of the car appeared to be . . . (complement—what?)
  vi. How can you remain . . . (complement—what?)
 vii. She certainly seemed . . . (complement—what?)
viii. She appeared . . . (adverb—how?)
  ix. Yesterday the bull broke . . . (object—what?)
   x. Yesterday the bull broke out . . . (adverb—where?)

In the passage from *The Swish of the Curtain* you will find inverted commas (or "quotation marks") used several times other than to indicate ordinary speech:

> their own "Blue Door Theatre"
> she felt excited and "wound up inside"
> she was pretending it was her first "first night"
> they felt "a bit het up"

Earlier in these Method Exercises, also, we have used them for single words, short phrases, etc., quoted from the sentences. What further uses of inverted commas, apart from marking conversation, seem to be illustrated here? In what sense does the term "quotation marks" fit all these uses of inverted commas?

Inverted commas can be used:

(a) to indicate direct speech;

(b) to refer to the title of a book, play, film etc. (printers often use italics for this);

(c) to call attention to any very particular or unusual name, including special places and buildings and curious nicknames;

(d) to indicate single words, phrases or sentences that are quoted from someone else, or from a book or other publication;

(e) to call attention to any unusual, rare, slang, foreign or made-up words used in writing.

Some printers use double inverted commas (" ") for use (a) and single (' ') for uses (b) to (e), but it is simpler to use double for them all, and reserve single for use when you wish to use inverted commas *inside* other inverted commas, e.g.:

"Have you ever read 'Treasure Island'?" Jean asked. Notice that in titles we also use capital letters for the first letters of the first word and all the other important words, but not for "the, of, in, a," etc., unless these are the first words of the titles.

Exercise 3. Justify the use of inverted commas in the following sentences, using the categories (a) to (e) above:
  i. When she says, "I know what I'm doing," she means it.
 ii. Pamela Brown wrote "Maddy Alone" and "Blue Door Venture" as well as "The Swish of the Curtain".
iii. He called his house "The Dungeon" and his cat was nicknamed "Warder Pete".
 iv. For "spoon" my little sister says "poon".
  v. "Weekend", "whisky" and "football" are all words the French have borrowed from the English.
 vi. The only "quote" he knew was "To be or not to be".

Exercise 4. Rewrite the following sentences including *all* the necessary punctuation. (But do *not* enclose complete answers in inverted commas.)
  i. the tale of two cities is a novel by charles dickens set in london and paris
 ii. in the play henry the fifth henry himself speaks the famous once more unto the breach speech
iii. in cockney rhyming slang plates of meat means feet and apples and pears are stairs
 iv. in gullivers travels we are told that the lilliputians called gulliver the man-mountain
  v. did you or did you not snapped the magistrate refer to the defendant as bandy-legs

Exercise 5. Practise the rules for writing in play form by continuing the following conversation about the actors' feelings before the opening concert at the "Blue Door Theatre". The conversation is based on the passage, but filled out so as to be more suitable for acting. Notice how names, stage directions, etc., are set out. (Underline instead of using italics.)

Do not rewrite this first scene of the conversation, but continue with another scene to take place back-stage in the theatre.

CHARACTERS: *Nigel Halford, Vicky and Bulldog Halford (the twins); Mr. Fayne and Sandra and Maddy, his daughters; Jeremy Darwin and Lyn, his sister.*

SCENE: *Outside the "Blue Door Theatre". Lyn, Sandra, Maddy and Jeremy (who carries a violin) are talking.*

LYN: I wish the others would hurry with that key. How do you feel, Maddy, nervous?

MADDY (*Sounding shivery and giving a nervous laugh*): No, not really. Just ordinary, really.

LYN: I'm sure all actors feel nervous before a first night, even the famous ones. I'm sort of wound up inside, as if something marvellous was going to happen. What about you, Sandra?

SANDRA: Yes, I feel worried, I must admit. Look, here are the Halfords.

(*Enter Nigel, Bulldog and Vicky.*)

LYN: Hullo, I hope you've remembered the key.

NIGEL: Of course I have. Here.

(*He gives it to Sandra.*)

SANDRA: Thanks. How do you three feel?

NIGEL: Oh, a bit het up, I suppose.

BULLDOG: So am I.

VICKY: (*laughing, to Bulldog*): You look like a beetroot!

SANDRA (*looking up at the sign before opening the theatre door*): Tons of people will be seeing this for the first time to-night. I wonder what they'll say? (*She opens the door. Exit into the hall.*)

JEREMY: It won't be much use if they're impressed with the theatre and disappointed by the actors.

(*They all enter the hall.*)

1. Have you any experience of acting, speaking or performing in public? Did you feel at all like any of the "Blue Door Theatre" players? Perhaps you have even more vivid memories of some other occasion which made you nervous—a serious interview with someone, or an occasion when you were in trouble or "on your best behaviour", or in the public eye. Recall the occasion, making notes on how you felt: begin with a simple list of all the symptoms of nervousness as you felt them (such as shivering, blushing, perspiring, looking pale, a tight or sick feeling in the stomach, and so on). Then plan your account of the occasion, with an introductory paragraph to explain what it was, a second paragraph to show how you came to be involved, and at least one paragraph to describe your own feelings of nervousness in detail. Think of an interesting way to round off the composition with a concluding paragraph.

2. Write a short composition in play form. The simplest would be a conversation or argument between two or three people. If you decide to tell a particular story, work out the details carefully, remembering that the story and the characters of the people involved, have to be unfolded almost entirely by what they say (and do) on stage. Avoid too many changes of scene, also, for these are distracting and boring for an audience.

A good single-scene plot would be that used in Jerome K. Jerome's amusing book "Three Men in a Boat", when he tells the fishing story of the prize trout in the glass case in the riverside public house. He and George enter the bar and ask an old man about the fish. He proudly tells them how he caught it. Enter the local carrier, who, when they tell him how they have been admiring the fish, tells them how he caught it! Enter another two local gentlemen, and they again claim to have caught the fish, as does the landlord. Finally, George climbs up for a better view, slips, clutches madly, and the case and fish are knocked to the floor and the fish broken into a thousand *plaster* fragments. It was not a stuffed trout at all!

1. Find out (with the help of books in the library) what the
following theatrical terms mean:

box-office success	back-cloth
good box-office	in the limelight
flies	a dais
wings	orchestra pit
floats or foots	stage manager
floods	producer or director
spots	green room
tabs	repertory
drapes	a review
front-of-house	a revue
down- and up-stage	critics
stage left and right	a lead
playing to the gallery	"to ham"
the gods	a cue
revolving stage	an understudy
proscenium (arch)	dress rehearsal
stalls or pit	prompt(er)
theatre in the round	properties

The Theatre by W. A. Lord and H. Webster (E.S.A.), 792 LOR,
is an example of a good, informative book with an index, and
a glossary of theatrical terms.

2. The class as a whole, or groups of the class, might try to
produce a play over the next few weeks. Decide first whether
it is to be "improvised" or acted from a complete script.
Groups should then work on several possible plots, and the
best (i.e. the most suitable to act) can then be chosen. Casting
must be done with care; it is often useful to have two people
learning the main part or parts, and to decide later who is to
take them, and who to "understudy". Scenery (though very
little is necessary), simple properties and costume have all to
be planned well in advance. Make sure that everyone in the
group or class has some part to play, on stage or off, and learns
it thoroughly. The success of a play depends on *everyone*.

3. Organize a group visit to the theatre at the first opportunity. Choose a suitable play for which you can get reasonably cheap seats, and telephone the theatre to see if you can book for any of the convenient afternoons or evenings, and whether they can offer any reductions for school parties. You will then have to write a business letter confirming the booking and enclosing a cheque or Postal Order and a stamped, addressed envelope. You may also be able to get reduced prices on the trains or buses to the theatre, if the party is large enough.

Books To Read

The Swish of the Curtain by PAMELA BROWN (Brockhampton)
The adventures of "the Blue Doors" do not end with their finding the theatre and putting on the concert. There are other shows, and then the final excitement of the drama contest, on which their future depends.
Devil-in-the-Fog by LEON GARFIELD (Longman; Penguin)
In the eighteenth century, 14-year-old George Treet lives and acts with a family group of strolling players; but adventure and mystery surround his right to be a proud nobleman.
White Boots by NOEL STREATFEILD (Collins; Penguin)
This book is about two very different girls who share the same ambition to be skating champions. The author makes you really care about what happens to all the characters, boys, girls and adults, in this exciting story.
Ballerina by NADA CURCIJA-PRODANOVIC (O.U.P.)
This book captures all the magic and mystery that surrounds the world of ballet. It follows the life of Lana from her entry into the Ballet School, with its hard work, laughter, quarrels, tragedy, encouragement and discipline from Miss Nina, until she emerges eventually as a ballerina.

The four Melendy children have a room to themselves at the top of the house where they live in New York with their father and "Cuffy", the housekeeper.

CHAPTER ELEVEN

A Room Of Your Own

The room in which they were sitting might have been called a playroom, schoolroom or nursery by most people. But to the Melendys it was known as the Office. It was at the very top of the house so that they could make almost all the noise they wanted to and it had everything such a room should have: a skylight and four windows facing east and north, and a fireplace with a basket-shaped grate. The floor was covered with scarred red linoleum that didn't matter, and the yellow walls were encrusted with hundreds of indispensable objects: bookcases bursting with books, pictures both by the Melendy children and less important grown-up artists, dusty Indian war bonnets, a string of Mexican devil masks, a shelf of dolls in varying degrees of decay, coats and hats hanging on pegs, the leftover decorations from Mona's birthday party, and other articles too numerous to mention. In one corner of the room stood an old upright piano that always looked offended, for some reason, and whose rack was littered with sheets of music all patched and held together with Scotch tape.

In addition to various chairs, tables and toy cupboards, there was a big dingy sofa with busted springs, a blackboard, a trapeze and a pair of rings. That was all but I think you will agree that it was enough. The Melendys seemed to go on and on collecting precious articles that they could never bear to throw away. The Office was their pride and joy, and what it lacked in tidiness it more than made up for in color and comfort and broken-down luxuries such as the couch and the piano. Also it was full of landmarks. Any Melendy child could have told you that the long scars on the linoleum had been made by Rush trying out a pair of new skates one Christmas afternoon; or that the spider-shaped hole in the east window had been accomplished by Oliver throwing the Milk of Magnesia bottle, or that the spark holes in the hearthrug had occurred when Mona tossed a bunch of Chinese firecrackers into the fire just for fun. Melendy history was written everywhere.

"There's that leak again," said Rush in a tone of lugubrious satisfaction. "It's getting bigger than it was last time even. Boy, will Cuffy be burned up!" He lay staring at the ceiling. "It's a funny shape," he remarked. "Like some kind of a big fat fish. And there's lots of other old dried-out leaks that have funny shapes. I can see a thing like a heart, and a thing like a baseball mitt, and a kind of lopsided Greyhound bus."

"You've missed Adolf Hitler, though," said Randy, thumping down off the trapeze and lying on the rug beside him. "See up there? That long fady line is his nose, and those two little chips are his eyes, and that dark place where you threw the plasticine is his moustache."

"I'm going to throw some more plasticine and make it into George Bernard Shaw," said Rush.

"Who's he?" inquired Randy.

"Oh, a man with a beard," said Rush. "I'd rather look at him than Hitler."

Mona put down her book.

"George Bernard Shaw is a playwright," she said. "My heavens, don't you even know *that*? He wrote a play called *Saint Joan*, all about Joan of Arc, that I'm going to act in someday."

"I bet's that's why you were walking round your room, holding the curtain rod out in front of you yesterday. You had kind of a moony expression and you kept talking to yourself. I thought to myself, she's gone goofy at last."

Rush shook his head and laughed appreciatively.

(from *The Saturdays* by Elizabeth Enright)

For Discussion

1. Give examples of the "color" and "comfort" in the room.
2. Were the skates roller-skates or ice-skates?
3. Explain: "Melendy history was written everywhere."
4. Do you think the piano and the music were much used?
5. Why might the piano have looked offended?
6. What does "lugubrious" mean? How does it apply to Rush's satisfied tone?
7. Why do you think Rush preferred George Bernard Shaw to Hitler?
8. What evidence can you find in this passage that it is about American children and by an American author?
9. What effects are obtained by using the following?
   (a) the yellow walls were *encrusted* (instead of "covered").
   (b) hundreds of *indispensable* objects (instead of "hundreds of objects").
   (c) whose rack was *littered* with sheets of music (instead of "covered").
   (d) had been *accomplished* by Oliver (instead of "made").
   (e) and laughed *appreciatively* (instead of "and laughed").
10. What are the advantages and disadvantages of having a children's room at the *top* of the house?
11. Do you think a child (or children) should always have a room to himself (or themselves)? Why? What kind of room is ideal for people of your age?

For Written Answers

1. Where were Rush and Randy at the opening of this passage?
2. Why would Cuffy be "burned up"?
3. What was Mona doing when Rush saw her on the previous day?
4. How much can you piece together about each of the four children? Write at least a sentence describing each.
5. Without looking again at the passage, describe the Melendys' "Office" in your own words, from memory.

Nelson Street

There is hardly a mouthful of air
In the room where the breakfast is set,
For the curtains are redolent yet
Of tobacco smoke, stale from last night.
There's the little bronze teapot, and there
The rashers and eggs on a plate,
And the sleepy canary, a hen,
Starts faintly her chirruping tweet,
And I know could she speak she would say:
"Hullo there — what's wrong with the light?
Draw the blind up, let's look at the day."
I see that it's Monday again,
For the man with the organ is there;
Every Monday he comes to the street
(Lest I, or the bird there, should miss
Our count of monotonous days)
With his reed-organ, wheezy and sweet,
And stands by the window and plays
"There's a Land that is Fairer than This."

SEUMAS O'SULLIVAN

148

Discussing The Poem

1. What details in this poem contribute to the idea that this is a depressing scene which is the same nearly every morning? Are there any pleasant or optimistic touches?
2. Why is the last line in inverted commas?
3. What do the following mean?

       redolent   rashers   monotonous   reed-organ

Method Exercises

In Book One we mentioned the use of *commas* to separate anything "aside" from the main sentence. Without looking at the passage or the poem, try to decide where commas were used in the following six short extracts from them:

   i. an old upright piano that always looked offended for some reason and whose rack was littered . . . .

  ii. a play called Saint Joan all about Joan of Arc that I'm going to act in . . . .

 iii. redolent yet of tobacco smoke stale from last night.

 iv. the sleepy canary a hen starts faintly her chirruping tweet . . . .

  v. lest I or the bird there should miss our count of monotonous days.

 vi. he comes . . . with his reed-organ wheezy and sweet and stands by the window . . . .

Commas were used here for three purposes:

(a) To divide off an adjective phrase which follows the noun it describes (except when introduced by "of"), as in:

He took her a cup of cocoa, thick and sweet with sugar, before she went to sleep.

(b) To divide off a word or phrase IN APPOSITION (which means "lying alongside"), that is, an alternative name or an explanatory phrase, as in:

Jean, Bill's elder sister, brought home a new umbrella, a red one with a black handle.

149

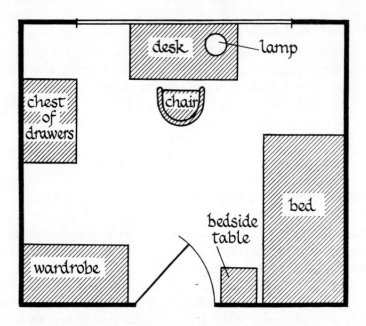

(c) To divide off a phrase IN PARENTHESIS, that is, an aside that might be in brackets.

She was hoping, not without reason, that she might break the long-jump record.

Which of the six extracts on page 149 illustrate each of these uses?

Exercise 1. Rewrite the following, inserting the commas that are necessary.

(a) Pat Peter's younger sister looked much older in a long satin dress trimmed with grey fur.

(b) Now just fourteen she sat nervously on the edge of her chair wondering what to say if one of Peter's noisy cheerful confident friends came over to talk to her.

(c) The children's room of course was full of previous souvenirs; there were battered books on the shelves an old guitar on the wall picture post-cards stuck above the beds a model aeroplane once the winner of a local competition suspended from the ceiling and a pair of rusty skates over the fire-guard.

(d) In 1603 Queen Elizabeth the last of the Tudors died and James I already King of Scotland succeeded her.

Exercise 2. In the passage, when Rush wants to describe the discoloured patch on the ceiling, he is naturally bound to compare it with something else. What does he compare it with? As we saw in Chapter 5, comparisons between different things are called *similes*. There is, of course, no point in comparing things that are identical, and if we compare really similar things (e.g. if we say that a girl is like her mother) these are called *literal comparisons*. To be effective, similes have to be fresh and original. Discuss the possible similes made by choosing one of the words in brackets in the following sentences. Are any of them literal comparisons? Which are the most original, interesting and effective similes?

(a) She sang like (a famous singer, a bird, the soothing voice of the sea).
(b) Oil dripped from the streaming machine like drops of (syrup, water, blood).
(c) The full moon moved across the hazy sky like (an eerie ghost, a little bent old man, a white saucer).
(d) The excavator crawled forward like (some prehistoric creature, a whale, an enormous tractor).
(e) Seen from the hill-top, the silvery river wound its way through the valley like (an eel, a Roman road, a shimmering necklace of pearls).
(f) She blushed like (a beetroot, a fiery furnace, anything).
(g) The feathers were as soft and pure as (silk, down, new-fallen snow).
(h) He was as slow as (his brother, he could be, a patient slug).
(i) The dark water sparkled in the sun like (neon signs, a glass of champagne, the Milky Way).
(j) Tugs were busy round the liner like (ducks on the water, kittens round their mother, bees round a honey-pot).
(k) His loud voice echoed angrily round the class-room like (a clap of thunder, solemn church bells, a howling dog).

Exercise 3. What are "synonyms"? Words of *opposite* meaning are called ANTONYMS. Often we can find an exact antonym, as with "black" and "white", but sometimes we cannot be so definite: the opposite of "lost" might be "found" or "saved", and the opposite of "rough" might be "smooth", "gentle" or "calm".

(a) Discuss possible antonyms for each of the following:

love	angry	perfect	supple	barren
diligent	solemn	clear	steep	wisdom

(b) Check all the meanings of the words in the following groups, and pick out the antonym in each group, from the synonyms.

e.g. request, ask, demand, beg, crave, <u>deny</u>.

   i. emperor, majesty, imperator, protector, president, subject.
  ii. witty, sullen, humorous, smart, waggish, facetious.
 iii. satirical, sarcastic, complimentary, critical, cynical, sardonic.
 iv. surcharge, rebate, reduction, discount, allowance, concession.
  v. savoury, dainty, palatable, appetizing, nauseous, delicious.
 vi. precede, succeed, antecede, forerun, presage, anticipate.
vii. entirely, completely, partially, altogether, wholly, fully.
viii. inception, conclusion, commencement, inauguration, beginning, opening.
 ix. alight, disembark, depart, return, arrive, reach.
  x. concern, grief, sorrow, distress, affliction, felicity.

Exercise 4. (a) All the following words are names of kinds of rooms.

Rearrange them in alphabetical order.

studio	cell	anteroom	scullery
mezzanine	galley	dressing-room	mess-room
refectory	boudoir	box-room	dormitory
saloon	lounge	salon	gallery
garret	cloak-room	box	pantry
nursery			

(b) Below there is one definition for each of the nouns in the above list. Rewrite the definitions, each with its appropriate noun.

> e.g. where a painter, sculptor or photographer works—
> studio.

   i. for young children to sleep and play in.

  ii. in which visitors wait to see someone important.

 iii. built into the roof of a house.

 iv. where guests can sit in a hotel.

  v. for changing clothes, especially in the theatre.

 vi. where outer garments can be left.

 vii. where a lady can find privacy.

viii. for a small private party at a theatre.

 ix. for storing cases, trunks, etc.

  x. for cooking, on a ship.

 xi. where a monk, nun, or prisoner lives.

 xii. where a Parisian lady of fashion entertained her guests.

xiii. for drinking in, in comfort.

xiv. for washing dishes, etc.

 xv. in which provisions are kept.

xvi. for eating in, especially in a college, etc.

xvii. where a company (of soldiers or sailors) eat together.

xviii. between two storeys, often low in height.

xix. containing a number of beds, especially in a boarding school.

 xx. for exhibiting works of art.

Exercise 5. Study this very exact description of a room:

The room measures four metres by three. It is on the first floor and there is one window, facing south and over-looking a garden. The door is in the centre of the opposite wall. In the corner on your right as you enter is a single bed with a small reading light over it, controlled by a pull-cord switch hanging from the ceiling above it. A small bedside table stands between the bed and the door. On your left as you enter, and facing the window, stands a large wardrobe, about one and a half metres across and two metres high, with a full-length mirror on its single door. Under the window is a writing desk and chair, with a table-lamp on the desk, and on the left-hand wall is a chest of drawers for clothes.

The walls are papered with a pattern of thin, vertical grey stripes on a white ground. The ceiling is grey, with a central light in a white glass globe. On the left-hand wall is a painting of a landscape with a lake and a steamer in it; and over the bed, on the right-hand wall, is a large notice-board, painted yellow, decorated mainly with pictures of sportsmen cut from magazines. There is a transistor radio on the chest of drawers and a cricket bat and pads stand in the corner to the right of the desk. The curtains are yellow with a delicate red pattern of stars, and the carpet, which covers nearly all the floor, is charcoal grey.

Notice that it gives the facts: first the position and size of the room, then the position of the main items of furniture, finally some details of decoration and smaller fixtures. It does not give opinions about how attractive the room is, nor is it a personal account of a visit to it and what happened there. It is the sort of description a police report might require.

Try to write a similarly factual and complete description of your own room or the class-room or some other room you know well. Use the same impersonal style.

Writing Your Own

In Exercise 5 you were writing as clearly and exactly as possible. For your composition you should be more personal and imaginative. Use original and striking similes and choose words with care. Plan the composition by thinking carefully about your room—real or ideal—and your reasons for liking it that way. This is important: ask yourself *why* you like particular furniture, equipment or colour schemes. Your ideas and reasons will keep the composition lively and personal.

Here are some suggested titles:

A Room of My Own.

My Ideal Room.

How I Would Furnish and Decorate a Room of My Own.

Why Every Teenager Should Have His Own Room.

The Design of an Ideal Kitchen (or Nursery, or Workshop, or Photographic Studio, etc.).

Things To Do

1. Prepare for a class discussion on housing and town-planning, taking the following questions into consideration:

whether garages should be provided for all houses and flats;

whether more people should be prepared to live in flats rather than houses;

whether more thought should be given to the needs of young children and old people (especially in designing flats);

whether all houses and flats should be built and owned by the government or local authorities, and not by private landlords letting them for profit;

whether towns should be re-planned so that large areas are free of cars;

whether parking charges in city centres should be made so expensive that motorists have to use public transport;

whether all houses and flats should be centrally-heated and air-conditioned.

2. Draw a plan (similar to that on page 150) or a picture to accompany your description in *Exercise* 5 or in the *Writing Your Own* section. Make it a clear plan or a colourful picture to help the reader visualize the room.

3. Write a poem about your room, or the view from your room or your home at some particular time of day, similar to the one in this chapter.

Your poem does not have to be about the room, or the view, in the daylight: you may like to let your imagination carry you away, as in this pupil's poem:

Holiday

Each and every night
I go for a short holiday;
Out through the window
I stare and wonder.

You may think
"This is no holiday,"
But to me it is.
A holiday from bustle,
Tussle and all care.

The exciting world of the free,
Cold air,
Trees and lights in the sky.
The sky is on fire!
In deep blue and orange aflare.

Excitement is wonder;
Wonder is not knowing, or doubt.
All my doubt is in six words,
"How did these things come about?"

PAUL

The Saturdays by ELIZABETH ENRIGHT (Heinemann; Penguin)
The Melendy children decide one wet Saturday to pool their pocket money so that each of them can go out in turn on successive Saturdays with a considerable sum to spend. Not all these expeditions are successful, but their later Saturdays, spent together, include some even greater disasters!

Peter's Room by ANTONIA FOREST (Faber & Faber)
Ginty is studying the Brontës and describes their imaginary kingdoms of Gondal and Angria. The Marlows decide to act a similar story in Peter's den, not realising that make-believe can be dangerous if taken too far.

Una and Grubstreet by PRUDENCE ANDREW (Heinemann; Penguin)
A baby's room in an empty house is just the refuge Una needs to save Christopher (or Ronnie) Heaven when she believes he has been battered by his mother. Una is eleven, motherly, worried about her father's new girl-friend, and she doesn't stop to consider the consequences of kidnapping someone's baby.

My Side of the Mountain by JEAN GEORGE (Bodley Head; Penguin)
Sam lives with his large family in New York, and decides to go and live alone in the Catskill Mountains. Taking only a pen-knife, an axe, a ball of string and flint and steel, he manages to look after himself in a hollow tree for over a year.

For a long time Ken McLaughlin has wanted a colt of his own and at last his father gives him permission to choose one from those on their ranch. A week later, Ken announces his choice to his father, mother and his brother, Howard.

CHAPTER TWELVE

I Really Want...

"*I'll take that sorrel filly of Rocket's; the one with the cream tail and mane.*"

Ken made his announcement at the breakfast table.

After he spoke there was a moment's astonished silence. Nell groped for recollection, and said, "A sorrel filly? I can't seem to remember that one at all—what's her name?"

But Rob remembered. The smile faded from his face as he looked at Ken. "*Rocket's filly*, Ken?"

"Yes, sir." Ken's face changed too. There was no mistaking his father's displeasure.

"I was hoping you'd make a wise choice. You know what I think of Rocket—that whole line of horses—"

Ken looked down; the colour ebbed from his cheeks. "She's fast, Dad, and Rocket's fast—"

"It's the worst line of horses I've got. There's never one amongst them with real sense. The mares are hellions and the stallions outlaws; they're untamable."

"I'll tame her."

Rob guffawed. "Not I, nor anyone, has ever been able to really tame any one of them."

Kennie's chest heaved.

"Better change your mind, Ken. You want a horse that'll be a real friend to you, don't you?"

"Yes—" Kennie's voice was unsteady.

"Well, you'll never make a friend of that filly. Last fall after all the colts had been weaned and separated from their dams, she and Rocket got back together—no fence'll hold 'em—she's all out and scarred up already from tearing through barbed wire after that bitch of a mother of hers."

Kennie looked stubbornly at his plate . . . .

"Well," McLaughlin barked. "It's your funeral—or hers. Remember one thing. I'm not going to be out of pocket on account of this—every time you turn around you cost me money—" . . . .

(*The colts are herded together in the corral. Then all except Ken's filly, Flicka, are driven out again.*)

But Flicka did not intend to be left. She hurled herself against the poles which walled the corral. She tried to jump them. They were seven feet high. She caught her front feet over the top rung, clung, scrambled, while Kennie held his breath for fear the slender legs would be caught between the bars and snapped. Her hold broke, she fell over backwards, rolled, screamed, tore around the corral.

One of the bars broke. She hurled herself again. Another went. She saw the opening, and as neatly as a dog crawls through a fence, inserted her head and forefeet, scrambled through and fled away, bleeding in a dozen places . . . .

Walking down from the corrals, Rob McLaughlin gave Kennie one more chance to change his mind. "Better pick a horse that you have some hope of riding one day. I'd have got rid of this whole line of stock if they weren't so damned fast that I've had the fool idea that someday there might turn out one gentle one in the lot, and I'd have a race horse. But there's never been one so far, and it's not going to be Flicka."

"It's not going to be Flicka," chanted Howard.

"Maybe she *might* be gentled," said Ken; and although his lips trembled, there was fanatical determination in his eye.

"Ken," said McLaughlin, "it's up to you. If you say you want her, we'll get her. But she wouldn't be the first of that line to die rather than give in. They're beautiful and they're fast, but let me tell you this, young man, they're *loco!*"

Ken flinched under his father's direct glance.

"If I go after her again, I'll not give up *whatever comes*, understand what I mean by that?"

"Yes."

"What do you say?"

"I want her."

"That's settled then," and suddenly Rob seemed calm and indifferent. "We'll bring her in again tomorrow or next day—I've got other work for this afternoon."

(from *My Friend Flicka* by Mary O'Hara)

For Discussion

1. Why did Ken want Flicka? What did he admire about her?
2. How did Ken's father know already that Flicka was a difficult filly?
3. This incident shows that Flicka was almost untamable: does it show any worthwhile qualities in the filly?
4. Why did Ken's lips tremble as they returned home? Why was he so determined?
5. What *did* Rob mean by "I'll not give up whatever comes"?
6. Explain the following:

sorrel	weaned and separated
colour ebbed from	from their dams
his cheeks	scarred up
hellions	a corral
guffawed	fanatical determination
last fall	indifferent

7. Why has the printer put the first line (of the passage itself, not the introduction), and some other words and short phrases, in italics? What would be the equivalent of these italics in handwriting?
8. Do you admire Ken's determination? Was he foolish or sensible in his attitude?
9. Would *you* have given in to Ken if you were in Rob's place? Should children have the things they really want?
10. What kind of treatment makes children "spoilt" and selfish?

1. What were the names of Ken's father and mother?
2. What do you think is meant by a horse being "loco"?
3. Explain in your own words what was wrong with this whole line of horses.
4. Why did Ken's father keep Rocket and her offspring at all?
5. Retell in your own words how Flicka broke out of the corral.

The Runaway

Once when the snow of the year was beginning to fall,
We stopped by a mountain pasture to say, "Whose colt?"
A little Morgan had one forefoot on the wall,
The other curled at his breast. He dipped his head
And snorted at us. And then he had to bolt.
We heard the miniature thunder where he fled,
And we saw him, or thought we saw him, dim and grey
Like a shadow against the curtain of falling flakes.
"I think the little fellow's afraid of the snow,
He isn't winter-broken. It isn't play
With the little fellow at all. He's running away.
I doubt if even his mother could tell him, 'Sakes,
It's only weather.' He'd think she didn't know!
Where is his mother? He can't be out alone."
And now he comes again with clatter of stone,
And mounts the wall again with whited eyes
And all his tail that isn't hair up straight.
He shudders his coat as if to throw off flies.
"Whoever it is that leaves him out so late,
When other creatures have gone to stall and bin,
Ought to be told to come and take him in."

ROBERT FROST

Discussing The Poem

1. What do you think the following mean?
   a little Morgan   sakes
   winter-broken   gone to stall and bin
2. Why do you think the colt behaved like this, first almost climbing the wall, then snorting, then running away and galloping back?
3. Is Frost sympathetic to the colt? Give examples of his close observation of the details of the colt and his behaviour.

Method Exercises

We have seen that most verbs need either an object or a subject complement to complete the sentence. What are the words in italics in the following examples—objects or complements?

> Ken wanted a *colt*.
> He chose *Flicka*.
> Flicka was a sorrel *filly*.
> She seemed a fast young *horse*.

Verbs that need a complement, however, may have an adjective as complement, instead of a noun:

> Flicka is a fast horse.
> Flicka is *fast*.
> Ken's father seemed a fierce man.
> His father seemed *fierce*.
> The grass became a wet marsh.
> The grass became *wet*.

163

Exercise 1. (a) Decide whether the following have noun (or pronoun) or adjective complements; and (b) rewrite each so that it becomes the other type, keeping the meaning approximately the same.

> e.g. His father was not a rich man. (noun complement)
> Answer: His father was not rich.

    i. The result of the match seemed a certainty.
   ii. She seemed very capable.
  iii. The house became a zoo full of animals.
   iv. The castle was ruined.
    v. The boy felt a fool.
   vi. The tree appeared to be rotten.
  vii. The play is a great success.
 viii. Some criminals turn honest men.
   ix. The explorer returned a disillusioned man.
    x. During the rescue, the night remained a calm one.

Exercise 2. What is an antonym? What is the antonym of "possible"? When searching for an antonym for "perfect", in the last chapter, did you choose "imperfect"? In both these cases the antonym can be formed by adding the letters -im before the word. In Book One we learnt that a group of letters (a syllable or syllables) added at the end of a word is called a *suffix*; a syllable added at the beginning is called a PREFIX. The following are common *antonym prefixes*:

in-, im-, un-, il-, ir-, dis-.

Perhaps the most common is un- (e.g. real: unreal).
Each of the above prefixes will fit two or more of the following twenty words. Rewrite the words with their antonym prefixes

> e.g. religious—irreligious
> legal—illegal
> honest—dishonest

happy	formed	curable	regular
logical	figure	patient	musical
appropriate	resolute	literate	order
qualify	gratitude	definite	mortal
readable	legible	appear	resistible

Exercise 3. We have seen how phrases can do the same work as adverbs and adjectives. Verbs also can consist of two or more words; in the passage we have:

> be able—Not I, nor anyone, *has* ever *been able* to really tame any one of them.
> get back—She and Rocket *got back* together.
> turn around—Every time you *turn around* you cost me money.
> get rid of—*I'd have got rid of* this whole line of stock.
> turn out—There *might turn out* one gentle one.
> give in—She wouldn't be the first to die rather than *give in.*
> go after—*I'll go after* her again.
> give up—*I'll* not *give up.*

These can be called PHRASAL VERBS. In the following exercise: (a) write out the verb in each sentence in full (in the first five the head-words of the verbs have been put in italics to help you); (b) choose the appropriate single-word verb from the list in brackets, and rewrite each sentence using the appropriate tense of single verb instead of the phrasal verb.

> e.g. The car was already taking up all the garage space.
>   (a) Verb: was . . . taking up
>   (b) The car *was* already *occupying* all the garage space.

(occupy; accommodate; succeed; surrender; accumulate; postpone; attack; criticise; quarrel; collect; remove.)

   i. The enemy soon *gave in.*
  ii. Mother could not *get* the stain *out.*
 iii. You have been *run*ning *up* a considerable debt.
  iv. The van *pick*ed *up* all our luggage at the station
   v. I shall be *put*ting my holiday *off* indefinitely.
  vi. She may well get on in her new job.
 vii. The dog was definitely going for the postman at the time
viii. They ran the plan down so much that few people believed in it.
  xi. Two friends like them would never fall out over such a trifle.
   x. The landlady cannot put up any more lodgers.

Exercise 4. Changing the position of an adverb in a sentence often alters the meaning of that sentence. Discuss the differences between the following:

Only last night she said she liked horses.
Last night she only said she liked horses.
Last night she said only she liked horses.
Last night she said she only liked horses.
Last night she said she liked only horses.

Changing the position of an adverb phrase in a sentence may also alter the meaning. Discuss these sentences:

In your best books now copy out the notes again.
Now copy out the notes in your best books again.
Now copy out the notes again in your best books.

Rewrite the following sentences altering (or improving) their meanings by moving an adverb or adverb phrase (or altering the punctuation). In the first five sentences the adverb or phrase has been printed in italics.

(a) The rebellion was crushed before any lives had been lost *by the army*.
(b) The candidate who had finished *quickly* left the room.
(c) He forgot to do the job *completely*.
(d) Fill up the scuttle which you will find in the cellar *with coke and anthracite*.
(e) *At least* the girls in the party knew how to cook.
(f) A criminal who steals often gets caught.
(g) Dogs only are admitted with their owners.
(h) Quick! Follow that man in a taxi.
(i) Lost: one small black kitten by an old age pensioner last seen with a red ribbon round her neck.
(j) This stone was erected in memory of Admiral James Jameson tragically killed in action by his fellow officers.

Exercise 5. Advertisers are very fond of using long, impressive, scientific terms in their advertisements, or giving the products technical names. Can you suggest some examples of this? In the following example, however, the trade name is in fact most inappropriate, although it *sounds* suitable:

> For small cuts and bruises, apply a little POLLUTION: the cream that soothes and cleanses.

Pollution, the dictionary tells us, means "uncleanness, impurity".

Explain why each of the following advertisements is equally inappropriate:

(a) Feeling tired, listless, lacking in energy? Try INERTIA tablets today.

(b) BLUNDERBUS, the wonderbus—the quietest, smoothest, safest way to travel.

(c) Massage no good? Friction inadequate? ELECTROCUTION is the *scientific* answer to your problems.

(d) For longer life, take RADIO-ACTIVE MALT, *daily*.

(e) The new VISOR-VISTA is the only car with the uninterrupted all-round vision.

(f) All the athletes say: "SOPORIFIC is terrific—for that extra effort that wins."

(g) *Our* sweets are nutty, nourishing and NOXIOUS.

(h) Beat, rhythm, harmony—discs of distinction, from CACA-PHONIC PRODUCTIONS, LTD.

(i) How to win friends and influence people—use a BLUDGEON, key to personal success.

(j) Are you ambitious? There is room at the top of *your* profession for the man who has taken a course in PROCRAST-INATION—the psychologist's answer to lack of self-confidence.

When you have explained all these, make up some more of your own on similar lines.

Writing Your Own

Have you ever wanted something as much as Ken did? Did you get it and, if so, how? Was it a struggle against opposition from your parents, or to find the money? Decide what is your most precious possession and write some notes about it: how you obtained it, any difficulties you had to overcome or sacrifices you had to make, and why you value it so highly. Then write a composition on one of these four topics:

How you obtained the possession.

Why you value the possession so highly.

The loss of your possession (whether you found it again, or not).

The one thing you would most like to have.

Whichever you choose, try to bring out your own feelings, and the tensions these may cause at home or inside yourself.

Things To Do

1. Horses (like dogs) have been so important a part of men's work and sport for thousands of years that many sayings and proverbs are connected with them. Here are a few examples:

Do not look a gift horse in the mouth. Do not change horses in mid-stream. You can take a horse to water, but you can't make him drink. To put (someone) through his paces. To spur (someone) on. At the end of one's tether. Horse-play. A slow coach. To put the cart before the horse. Neck and neck.

Explain the meaning and use of each of these; and see how many more you can collect (and explain).

2. Groups or individuals could make a folder or book entitled *The Horse*. Chapters should include the horse's early domestication and breeding, horses in battles and campaigns of the past, the development of harness and cavalry equipment, the history of horse-drawn vehicles, pack-horses, farm-horses and race horses, well-known horse stories and books, stables and accommodation, famous horse-men and women and jockeys, pony-trekking and polo, the horse in ceremony and pageantry, and so on.

In the library, use reference books and books under reference numbers: 636.1 (domestic animals), 599.7 (zoology), 798 (horsemanship), 357 (cavalry, military science), 385 (transport), etc.

3. Many people are eager to learn how to ride and to look after their own horse or pony. Plan either a riding school, or the best accommodation for keeping a private pony. In either case draw diagrams and prepare a manual of advice on the care of the animal(s) or the art of learning to ride.

Books To Read

My Friend Flicka by MARY O'HARA (Methuen; Mayflower)
Flicka is finally captured, but, as if to prove Rob McLaughlin's statement that she would die rather than give in, she very nearly kills herself in attempting to escape.
The Yearling by MARJORIE KINNAN RAWLINGS (Heinemann; Penguin)
The yearling in this famous story is a fawn which young Jody Baxter saves and rears, on his father's homestead in Florida. But their life is hard and dangerous, and in the end he has to face the terrible decision to shoot the yearling that he has loved and cared for.
A Dog So Small by A. PHILIPPA PEARCE (Longman; Penguin)
Although he lives in London, Ben longs for a dog. His grandfather promises him one for his birthday, but he receives what seems to be a polished woodwork picture of the smallest dog of the smallest breed in the world. This starts Ben's mind working and begins a strange adventure that ends in Ben's having a real dog of his own.
The Spuddy by LILLIAN BECKWITH (Hutchinson)
This is the story of an independent mongrel dog, The Spuddy, befriended by Andy and then by Jake, skipper of the fishing boat "Silver Crest". In the final tragedy, The Spuddy shows his heroic quality and Andy, till then dumb, finds he can speak.

*Three Polish children, Ruth, Edek and Bronia, accompanied by their
friend Jan, are journeying to Switzerland to find their father, who had
fled there after escaping from a Nazi prison camp. They travel part of the
way in two canoes; but then the girls lose their only paddle and their
canoe becomes grounded.*

CHAPTER THIRTEEN

On The River

And they sat there shivering and clinging to each other till the shadows brightened and they could see the whole sweep of the river, white and broken in the middle, rock-strewn and shallow at either side, with the wood-muffled hills hemming it in, and not a soul in sight. No sign of Edek and Jan. They could not have felt lonelier.

Then Bronia saw something which gave them hope. Down in the water, near the point of the V-shaped rock, was a stick that looked as if it might serve as a paddle. She climbed down to get it and found it was the very paddle they had lost. This was luck indeed.

They turned the canoe over and poured the water out. Then, with new confidence, they launched it again. Stepping aboard, they headed for midstream. And the current caught them and carried them on towards the rapids.

The river grew faster, and the bank flashed past. Soon they were in a kind of gorge, where the river squeezed past great boulders, some of them as high as houses. Some of the swells were over a foot high, and the spray dashed over the bow and stung their faces. The water roared here so that even the loudest shout could not be heard. Out to the left there were huge oily surges that looked as if they would pound you down into the depths if you got caught in them.

Bronia closed her eyes and clung to her sister's waist. Ruth was not as scared as she had expected to be. With a triumphant sense of exhilaration she flashed in with her paddle, heading always for the open stream, away from the white broken water where the rocks lay hidden. Now and then a boulder loomed up and she knew that if they struck it they would be dashed to pieces. But a quick dip of the paddle at the right moment was enough to shoot them safely past.

In no time the river broadened, the boulders eased, and the banks were wooded again. The terrors of the rapids were over. Ruth hoped that Edek and Jan, whose two-seater was much less easy to manoeuvre, had been as successful as they had.

There seemed no need for the paddle now, for the water was clear of rocks and the current smooth and swift. They could lie back and let the canoe take care of itself.

Bronia closed her eyes and fell asleep. Ruth lay back and watched the blue sky overhead and the climbing sun. It was to be another scorching day, and she too became sleepy and dozed.

A grating, tearing sound brought her to her senses, and she woke to find herself thigh-deep in water. The canoe had grounded on a shoal and a sharp stone had ripped the canvas underneath. She looked about her. The river was very broad here, and they were near the right bank, where it was shallow and easy to wade ashore. So they stepped out and scraped the waterlogged craft over the pebbles to the bank and hauled it ashore.

(from *The Silver Sword* by Ian Serraillier)

For Discussion

1. Why were the girls "shivering and clinging to each other"?
2. Which of the girls was the older?
3. Is there any evidence in this passage to suggest that they had been canoeing at night?
4. Was it summer or winter? How do you know?
5. Do you imagine that the girls' canoe was larger or smaller than the boys'?
6. Why was Ruth not "as scared as she expected to be"?
7. Was it really true that they could "let the canoe take care of itself" once they were past the rapids?
8. What do the following mean here?

   hemming it in   exhilaration   a shoal
   the swells   to manoeuvre   waterlogged

9. What effects are obtained by using the following?
   (a) the *wood-muffled* hills (instead of "woods and hills")
   (b) the river *squeezed* past great boulders (instead of "flowed")
   (c) huge *oily surges* (instead of "waves")
   (d) would *pound* you down (instead of "pull")
   (e) she *flashed in with* her paddle (instead of "dipped")
   (f) a boulder *loomed up* (instead of "appeared")
   (g) *scraped* the waterlogged craft (instead of "pulled" it)
10. Is canoeing a dangerous pastime? What precautions or training are necessary? What are its advantages as a sport?

For Written Answers

1. Were they travelling upstream or down? Give a reason for your conclusion.
2. If the rocks in the rapids "lay hidden", how did Ruth pick them out?
3. What was Ruth using the paddle for in the rapids?
4. Why did the girls feel tired?
5. How did Ruth come to find herself thigh-deep in water?

From: *The Cataract of Lodore*

The cataract strong then plunges along;
Striking and raging as if a war raging
Its caverns and rocks among;
Rising and leaping, sinking and creeping,
Swelling and sweeping, showering and springing,
Flying and flinging, writhing and wringing,
Eddying and whisking, spouting and frisking,
Turning and twisting, around and around
With endless rebound: smiting and fighting
A sight to delight in, confounding, astounding,
Dizzying and deafening the ear with its sound:
Collecting, projecting, receding and speeding,
And shocking and rocking and darting and parting,
And threading and spreading and whizzing and hissing,
And dripping and skipping and hitting and splitting,
And shining and twining and rattling and battling,
And shaking and quaking, and pouring and roaring,
And moaning and groaning:
And glittering and frittering, and gathering and feathering,
And whitening and brightening, and quivering and
shivering,
And flurrying and scurrying, and thundering and
floundering;
Delaying and straying and playing and spraying,
Advancing and prancing and glancing and dancing,
Recoiling, turmoiling and toiling and boiling,
And flapping and rapping and clapping and slapping,
And curling and whirling and purling and twirling,
And thumping and bumping and jumping,
And dashing and flashing and splashing and clashing,
And so never ending, but always descending,
Sounds and motions for ever and ever are blending
All at once and all o'er, with a mighty uproar;
And this way, the water comes down at Lodore.

ROBERT SOUTHEY

Discussing The Poem

1. Examine the rhymes used in this poem: notice when one line rhymes with the following one or with one several lines below, and when one half of a line rhymes with the other half, and so on. Why does Southey vary his rhyme pattern? Why are some lines longer than others?
2. What is the effect of using so many words ending in -ing? Is this appropriate to describe a waterfall?
3. Pick out words in the poem where the sound represents the meaning, as with "hissing" and "splashing".

Method Exercises

Examine the structure of the poem: would you say that these lines are describing *how* the water falls down, or do they describe the waterfall? Now examine these four examples:

> I watched the leaves *quivering in the breeze.*
> The *quivering* leaves were very beautiful.
> John stood there *quivering with excitement.*
> He *was quivering* all over.

In the first, the phrase in italics is definitely an adjective phrase: "quivering" describes the leaves, not how I watched them. Similarly, "quivering" is an adjective in the second. In the third, the phrase could be adjectival (describing John) or adverbial (how John stood). It is possible in the last example to maintain that "quivering" is an adjective complement (as you might say: "John was *brown* all over"), but it is simpler to call it part of the verb "to quiver" (John quivers, John quivered, John was quivering, etc.).

Thus, words formed from verbs and ending in -ing can be:

    i. part of some tenses of the verb,
    ii. single adjectives,
    iii. part of adjective phrases,
    iv. adverbs or part of adverb phrases.

These words are called PRESENT PARTICIPLES of verbs.

Exercise 1. Which of the four uses given overleaf does each of the present participles printed in italics below, represent?

e.g. The tourist was *talking* to the bishop.

Talking=part of the past tense of "to talk".

The Polish children are *journeying* to Switzerland.

(a) They sat there, *shivering* and *clinging* to each other.

(b) They were *clinging* to each other.

(c) *Stepping* aboard, they headed for midstream.

(d) The captain is *stepping* aboard now.

(e) Ruth flashed in with her paddle, *heading* always for the open stream.

(f) Ruth watched the *climbing* sun.

(g) Ruth watched the sun *climbing*.

(h) It was to be another *scorching* day.

(i) A *grating, tearing* sound brought her to her senses.

(j) We are *discussing* the poem.

(k) My friend had been *thinking* of buying a canoe.

(l) I am *hoping* for some help with this exercise.

Present participles are the cause of two very common kinds of mistakes. First, it is easy to confuse a present participle with a complete verb. It is only part of a verb, and requires words like "am, is, are, was, were, have been," etc. (part of the verb "to be") to make it complete. A present participle is therefore *not* sufficient to complete a statement sentence; e.g.

People rushing, pushing and stumbling down the steps, all in an unreasonable hurry to get home.

still needs a verb to complete it:

People *were* rushing . . . .   People *are* rushing . . . .

Secondly, present participles and phrases introduced by present participles are always assumed to describe the nearest noun (or pronoun), especially if this is the subject of the sentence. Thus:

Riding her cycle down the road, a dog dashed under Jane's wheel.

means that the dog was riding Jane's bicycle! How should this be rewritten to make the intended meaning clear?

Exercise 2. Rewrite the following, making sufficient alterations or additions to say correctly what the author meant to say.

e.g.　　Whilst reading a book in the garden, a fly got into Paul's eye.

Answer: Whilst Paul was reading a book in the garden, a fly got into his eye.

(a) Weeping sadly they found the poor little child alone.
(b) Entering the cave, the smell was quite overpowering.
(c) Three little children playing hop-scotch in the street.
(d) We flew over the Statue of Liberty flying from London to New York.
(e) The old man, having three sons and no daughters, and wanting to provide for his own old age.
(f) Crossing the Strait of Dover the sea was very rough.
(g) On all sides men laughing, children playing, women gossiping and on the stand the band playing lively military music.
(h) After reading his latest book, Ian Serraillier is certainly one of my favourite authors.
(i) The queue of people waiting for their turn.
(j) Returning home late last night, the stars were very beautiful.

Exercise 3. (a) Much of the effect of the extract from *The Cataract of Lodore* is due to the rhyme. Rhyming words at the ends of lines has for centuries been common in English verse, and rhymes follow different patterns: for instance, couplets, where one line is rhymed with the next:

This books can do—nor this alone: they give	a
New views to life, and teach us how to live;	a

and quatrains, where alternate lines rhyme:

Beneath this stone, a lump of clay,	a
Lies Uncle Peter Dan'els,	b
Who, early in the month of May,	a
Took off his winter flannels.	b

Notice how "code letters" can be used to indicate a rhyme scheme.

How are the lines rhymed in Southey's poem on page 174? Do they follow any regular pattern? Is rhyme ever used *within* the lines, or so that a last word in one line rhymes with one in the middle of a later line?

(b) Rhymes are similar sounds repeated at the end of the word. In English we also have a very strong and ancient tradition of ALLITERATION, the repetition of consonant sounds, especially at the *beginning* of words.

Flying and flinging, writhing and wringing,

is an example in the poem, where fl- and wr- are repeated. What other examples are to be found in the lines from *The Cataract of Lodore*?

Many of our popular sayings and phrases are alliterative: see if you can complete, and then write out, the following:

e.g. bag and baggage   neck or nothing

bread and	from top to	now or . . . .
bed and	as large as	as pleased as . . . .
safe and	at sixes and	as right as . . . .
to kill or	rack and	as thick as . . . .
as bold as	with might and	the more the . . . .
as dead as	rough and	slow but . . . .
penny wise		

Exercise 4. Alliteration often reinforces the meaning of words by the impression of their sound. When words are formed *directly* from the sounds of things or actions, this is called ONOMATOPOEIA;

    e.g.   splash   snap   click   tinkle

are words representing sounds and actually *sounding like* what they represent.

The same term, *onomatopoeia,* is applied to using the sounds of *any* words or phrases to imitate particular noises. Can you find an example in the extract from *The Cataract of Lodore?* Here is one from Dylan Thomas's poem *Fern Hill:*

    . . . the foxes on the hills barked clear and cold.

(a) What creatures might make each of these noises?

neigh	moo	cluck	howl
bray	bleat	cheep	buzz
gobble	caw	chirp	hum
growl	coo	twitter	hoot
snarl	purr	bellow	squeal

(b) Make up the most lively and interesting sentences you can using the following onomatopoeic words. e.g. *wheeze*:

The vintage pump engine coughed, wheezed and thumped as water gushed from the pipe.

| clatter | clash | patter | rustle | sizzle |
| blast | plump | whirr | clack | wail |

(c) Make a list of as many more onomatopoeic words as you can think of.

Exercise 5. In Chapter Two we discussed an exact description of a room. After studying the diagrams below, write an exact description of how boats are raised and lowered on a canal by means of locks. Do *not* make this a personal story. Your aim is to give a clear and exact account, in logical order, of how *any* lock would work. Begin by saying what a lock is for, and describe a typical one. Then explain the process, making it clear how the gates are held closed by water pressure, how the water level can be raised and lowered in the lock, and how the gates themselves are opened and closed.

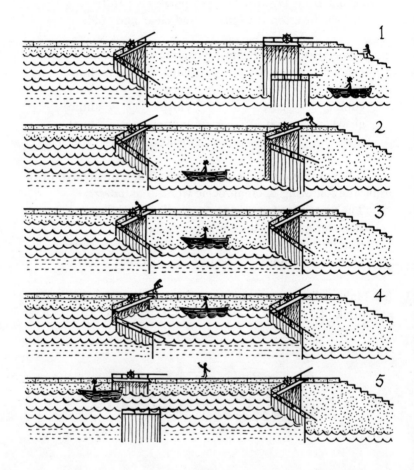

Writing Your Own

Most people find water fascinating. Discuss briefly what is particularly attractive about (a) still, calm water, (b) strong, flowing, deep water, (c) rapid, turbulent water, (d) falling water. Do you like watching ripples, foam, spray, eddies, whirlpools, fountains or the wake of a ship? Watch a drop of water forming on and then falling from a slowly dripping tap, or the current dragging water weeds in a stream or river. Make a list of comparisons that seem effective, and a list of words that describe the sight, sound or feel of water.

Write a description of any riverside or waterside scene. Choose *any* river, stream or lake scene that you know, and decide on the weather, the time of day and year, the number of people about, and so on. Write as clear and as vivid an account of the water as you can. If you wish, write about the river traffic—boats, visitors, fishermen, etc.—but pay special attention to the beauty and fascination of the water itself, and of the trees and water weeds, birds and fish, by, on or in the water. Remember to write in paragraphs.

Things To Do

1. What are the three longest rivers in the British Isles? Find out what you can about them, perhaps using this information to draw a map showing their courses and the most important or interesting riverside towns, together with notes about historical events or existing places of interest associated with the rivers.

2. Alternatively, if you live near any fairly large river, you should be able to collect much interesting information about it. For instance, what industries are found on its banks, and how have these changed over the centuries? Who built the bridges, and when? What authority is responsible for keeping the river clean and the banks in good condition? What is the fishing like? How much water traffic (including pleasure craft) is there? Does the water feed reservoirs? Are there locks, fords, weirs, waterfalls or rapids? What historic scenes have been associated with the river? What wild life and plant-life are to be found?

All this might well be enough to occupy the whole class in visits and research and in map-making, illustrations and writing up factual information. One number of the class magazine could be devoted entirely to this theme.

3. Prepare an illustrated talk to the class on one of the following subjects. (The library section 797 includes nearly all the water-sports; some other library reference numbers are given in brackets.)

Yachting	Water fowl (598.2)
Rowing	Fishers and waders (598.2)
The Boat Race	River fishing (799)
Henley Regatta	Swans and "swan-upping" (598.2)
Enjoying canoeing	"Three Men in a Boat"
Building a canoe	Paddle-boats and other pleasure-boats
Canoe holidays	
Sailing a dinghy	Water buses and ferries
Holidays afloat	Trees of the river bank (582)
Thames barges (623)	Mammals on the river bank (599)
Water skiing	Water supplies of cities (628.1)
Speed boats (623)	Locks, dams and weirs (626)
Hovercraft (623)	The world's finest bridges (624)
Hydrofoils (623)	Tunnelling beneath rivers (624)
Punting	Soft and hard water (551)

The Silver Sword by IAN SERRAILLIER (Cape; Heinemann; Penguin)
This exciting story of how the four children trekked across
war-devastated Europe, from Poland to Switzerland, is based
on fact. And it can be enjoyed equally by boys and girls.

The Boy and the River by HENRI BOSCO (translated by Gerard
Hopkins) (O.U.P.)
Pascalet lives near a river in Southern France, where his
parents have forbidden him to play. But he hears about the
river's attractions from a poacher, finds a boat and meets
another boy, Gatzo, on an island. They row off to explore a
network of remote waterways. *The Fox in the Island* is a sequel
to this book, with an even stranger air of mystery.

The Dolphin Crossing by JILL PATON WALSH (Macmillan; Penguin)
Of this exciting story based on Dunkirk in 1940, the author
wrote: "There really were schoolboys who joined the many
civilians in ferrying the British army back across the Channel. I
hope this is also a truthful book in another sense; when real
people take real risks, they really get killed."

The Machine-Gunners by ROBERT WESTALL (Macmillan)
A gang of tough schoolchildren from a Tyneside town find a
machine-gun during the Blitz and decide to wage their own
war against Germany.

Karen Forest loves to play the piano. On Saturday afternoons she visits Aunt Anne who helps her to practise. During the week she has permission, through Miss Hemans who cleans the Parish Hall, to use an ancient piano stored in its kitchen.

CHAPTER FOURTEEN

Music

Karen learnt all the pieces in the instruction book quickly, but, Aunt Anne was afraid, chiefly by ear.

"You mustn't do that. You mustn't look at your hands. I remember I was never allowed to look at my hands," she said, worriedly, and caused a friend of Mrs. Bent's, who was a carpenter, to make a board that fitted the keyboard of her piano from end to end. It was supported by uprights, six inches high, at each end, and under that canopy Karen's hands had to creep and crawl, finding their way to the right notes by themselves, as it were. That was how Aunt Anne had practised during a happy year of her girlhood, when she had gone away to "finish" and had had lessons. It had, she declared, done her a great deal of good.

The board taught Karen to read. She looked at her music because there was nothing else to look at, and Aunt Anne, by the simple method of giving a scream whenever she played a wrong note, taught her to listen to herself. The lessons were not orthodox. Aunt Anne never sat down beside her pupil. She never appeared, in fact to be giving any attention, but wherever she happened to be—in the garden with her hoe, or upstairs turning out a drawer—she heard. "Ow! B flat, not B natural," she would bawl. "Can't you hear? Listen to yourself for goodness' sake!" And Karen, who, as a matter of fact could hear perfectly when she tried, would hastily correct herself under the board, being careful not to scrape the skin off her knuckles against its rough surface. Mrs. Bent's friend, who had done it cheaply, had not wasted his money on sandpaper . . . .

She was supremely happy on her Saturday afternoons. The

lessons consisted of scales for ten minutes and after that any-thing she liked. Like a bee gathering honey she turned over the leaves of most of the music in the cabinet beside the piano, taking a sip here and there wherever it looked easy, storing up lovely tunes, as she had once stored up *Drink*, with which to regale Miss Hemans later on.

Miss Hemans was not very discriminating; as an audience that was her only fault.

"Listen to this, Hemsey" (the "miss" was not long in dis-appearing), "it's the tune out of the Beethoven violin concerto. Aunt Anne says it's the most heavenly tune in the whole world. Or "Listen to this one; Mrs. Bent always asks for it. It's called *Tea for Two*." And Miss Hemans would duly listen and invariably remark: "Ever s'nice, isn't it?" All the tunes were nice, just as the weather was nice or a cup of tea was nice when one had scrubbed the floor. All the same she was a real audience; she listened. "I've 'ad that one," she would say, sourly, if Karen played something twice through. Also it was most gratifying the way she was everlastingly impressed that Karen could produce such sounds at all. "I couldn't do it, not if I were to try ever so," she would say, truthfully enough, as she shut down the lid of the piano; and Karen, her cheeks bulging with toffee, would dance happily home secure in her little possessions—a row of tunes that were her own, that people like Miss Hemans could only have if they asked for them.

(from *She Shall Have Music* by Kitty Barne)

For Discussion

1. What does "by ear" mean? What is wrong with learning to play an instrument only by ear?
2. Why is it a good idea to avoid looking at your hands when learning (a) to play the piano, and (b) to type?
3. What other important lesson had Karen to learn, as well as how to read the music?
4. Do you think Aunt Anne was an accomplished musician herself?
5. What does "discriminating" mean? What does it mean to say that Miss Hemans was "not very discriminating"?
6. Why do people have to practise scales when learning to play an instrument? What else does a musician have to learn?
7. Do you think Karen had any musical talent? Give reasons for your opinion.
8. What do the following mean?

canopy	to regale	invariably
to "finish"	concerto	gratifying
orthodox	duly	

9. What kinds of music do the *Beethoven Violin Concerto* and *Tea for Two* represent? How many different kinds of music can you list? What tune could *Drink* be?
10. What do you think makes music so universally popular? Why should people want to be able to compose, play and listen to music at all?

For Written Answers

1. What were Aunt Anne's methods as a music teacher?
2. Why did Karen like playing to Miss Hemans?
3. How musical was Miss Hemans?
4. What is the most important feature of a good audience?
5. What signs are there that Karen's family could not afford to have her expensively trained as a musician?

Music Comes

Music comes
Sweetly from the trembling string
When wizard fingers sweep
Dreamily, half asleep;
When through remembering reeds
Ancient airs and murmurs creep,
Oboe oboe following,
Flute answering clear high flute,
Voices, voices—falling mute,
And the jarring drums.

At night I heard
First a waking bird
Out of the quiet darkness sing . . .
Music comes
Strangely to the brain asleep!
And I heard
Soft, wizard fingers sweep
Music from the trembling string,
And through remembering reeds
Ancient airs and murmurs creep;

Oboe oboe following,
Flute calling clear high flute,
Voices faint, falling mute,
And low jarring drums;
Then all those airs
Sweetly jangled—newly strange,
Rich and change . . .
Was it the wind in the reeds?

Did the wind range
Over the trembling string:
Into flute and oboe pouring
Solemn music; sinking soaring
Low to high,
Up and down the sky?
Was it the wind jarring
Drowsy far-off drums?

Strangely to the brain asleep
Music comes.

JOHN FREEMAN

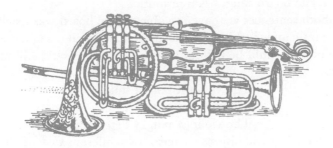

Discussing The Poem

1. Look carefully in this poem for (a) whole lines repeated,
   and (b) single words repeated (often within the same line).
   Discuss the reasons for their repetition, and also the reasons
   for any slight changes. What effect does the poet wish to
   achieve?

2. What different kinds of instrument seem to be represented
   here? Is this a complete "cross-section" of musical instruments?

3. Discuss the words the poet uses, particularly the adjectives:
   why are strings "trembling", or reeds "remembering", or
   drums "jarring"? Would you call these examples of onomatopoeia?

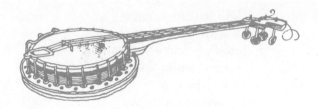

Method Exercises

Karen learnt all the pieces.

This is a simple statement sentence. What are the subject, verb and object? Now try to decide what are subjects, verbs and objects of the following:

The board had done Aunt Anne a lot of good.

The board taught Karen music.

In both sentences we have *two* objects: the board was teaching (a) music and (b) Karen. Indeed, in many such cases, either of the objects could be left out and the sentence would still make sense.

The violinist taught music.

The violinist taught Peter.

The violinist taught Peter music.

Of course, by two objects we mean two different *kinds* of object; contrast the following, where the objects are plural, with the sentences above:

The violinist taught music and dancing.

The violinist taught Peter and Mary.

The violinist taught Peter and Mary music and dancing. A number of verbs frequently take two objects: give, lend, find, tend, bring, ask, tell, promise, are all examples. The objects are of different kinds: one is the normal object, what is given, lent, found, etc., and is called the DIRECT OBJECT. The other is usually the person (or people) to whom or for whom it is given, lent, found, etc., and is called the INDIRECT OBJECT. (But note that if the words "to" or "for" are used before the person, it is no longer called an object of the verb:

The violinist taught music to Peter.

"Peter" is *not* called the indirect object of "taught".)

Exercise 1. Write out (in 4 columns) the subject, verb, indirect object and direct object of the following sentences:

SUBJECT	VERB	INDIRECT OBJECT	DIRECT OBJECT
e.g. Karen	played	Miss Hemans	a tune

(a) Her mother gave her a beautiful necklace.
(b) I can lend you twenty pence.
(c) Miss Hemans found Karen a piano.
(d) The class will send the children's home a cheque.
(e) My uncle brought me a souvenir.
(f) Will you ask the speaker another question?
(g) The Headmaster promised the school a half-holiday.
(h) May we offer your friend a drink?
(i) That experience taught the boys a lesson.
(j) New members have to pay the treasurer an entrance fee.

Word order alone tells us whether a noun is subject, direct object or indirect object. Identify the subjects and objects in these sentences:

The home-help insulted the supervisor.

We gave the home-help a new supervisor.

We also gave the supervisor a new home-help.

When we use pronouns instead of nouns, we change many of them according to whether they are subject or object. (There is no difference between the direct and indirect object forms.) Write down the object forms of these pronouns:

I, you, he, she, it, we, you, they.

Turn to page 92 to check that you are correct.

In addition, the pronoun "who" (which is used to ask questions and to introduce adjective phrases and clauses) has an object form "whom", e.g.

Who wants to come? (subj.)

Whom do you want? (obj.)

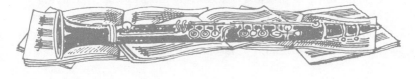

191

Exercise 2. The subject and object forms of pronouns are often confused. Each of the following sentences includes one misused pronoun. Rewrite them, correcting this mistake.

      e.g.   Shall us all help him do it?

      Answer: Shall *we* all help him do it?

(a) Jim and me want to start a new youth club.

(b) All us boys are very keen on it.

(c) Him and his friends will not support us in our venture.

(d) Who will help us and who can we help?

(e) The people who we want to help really do need us.

(f) Please give Jim and I all the support you can.

(g) It was me who first thought of the scheme.

(h) When we all took part, whom should take the credit?

(i) He and his friends will never be as successful as us.

(j) It was they who we very much wanted to beat.

Exercise 3. To Miss Hemans everything was "nice". She was a woman of very limited vocabulary! What words might she have used to describe more accurately the violin concerto, *Tea for Two*, the weather, and a cup of tea after scrubbing the floor? In the following conversation, Mrs. A and Mrs. B both have very limited vocabularies: each has *two* favourite words to cover almost every description—what are they? In all there are thirty inadequate adjectives and adverbs in the conversation. Replace these with better, more accurate ones, using those in the list below if you wish. (Try not to use the same word more than once.)

absorbing	delicious	distressing	great	sheer
beautiful	delightful	enjoyable	grim	successful
charming	depressing	excessively	interesting	terrifying
cheerful	difficult	extremely	miserably	uncomfort-
comfortable	disgusting	fine	picturesque	able
complete	dismal	fascinating	pleasant	unusually
				welcome.

MRS. A: Did you have a nice time at that nice place by the sea?

MRS. B: Not really. The boarding house was lovely and they gave us lovely food, but the weather was awful. The children were awful because they were bored and it was such an awful strain trying to think of something lovely to do each awful morning. I was awfully glad to get back for a lovely rest!

MRS. A: How terrible! It was not terribly nice here last week, I suppose, but we had a very nice afternoon on Thursday on that nice outing with the Guild. The coach-ride was terrible because I always feel terribly sick in coaches. But the castle was nice. There was a nice guide who told us all the castle's terrible history, and then we had a nice tour of the museum with those terrible instruments of torture.

MRS. B: It sounds lovely. We saw a lovely castle on the television. It was not awfully old, but it was on a lovely cliff overlooking a lovely river. We could have had a lovely holiday there, I'm sure, although I expect the plumbing is awful.

Exercise 4. (a) Try to define the following musical terms:
   i. recital, concert, opera, session, musical comedy.
   ii. melody, rhythm, harmony, discord, motif, movement.
   iii. solo, duet, trio, quartet, quintet, sextet.

(b) Make three columns, headed nouns, adjectives and verbs, and in each put all the words you can collect that describe musical sounds, or noises in general; a start has been made for you. As you will see, the words in one column do not necessarily have to correspond exactly with words in the others.

NOUNS	ADJECTIVES	VERBS
blare	resonant	to blare
flourish	loud	to resound
thump	muffled	to deaden
hiss	hissing	to hiss

Exercise 5. Without referring to the passage, decide where an apostrophe should appear in the following, all taken from the passage; in one, no apostrophe is required:

You mustnt do that	Mrs. Bents friend
a friend of Mrs. Bents	its the most heavenly tune
cant you hear?	ever snice, isnt it?
for goodness sake!	Ive ad that one
against its rough surface	I couldnt do it

Turn back to Chapter Five if you are still unsure about using the apostrophe.

Explain why there are inverted commas round "finish" (2nd paragraph of the passage) and "miss" (6th paragraph). What would be the equivalent in ordinary handwriting of the italics the printer used for *Tea for Two* (last paragraph)? Turn back to Chapter Ten if you are uncertain about these uses of inverted commas.

In rewriting the following paragraph, you have to insert capital letters (some have been put in for you), one set of inverted commas, commas, full-stops and apostrophes.

Schuberts Eighth Symphony known as the unfinished wasnt in fact left unfinished for any obvious reasons such as the composers death two of the composers friends Joseph and Anselm Hüttenbrenner had had him elected an honorary member of a famous musical society and in 1823 he sent anselm this uncompleted symphony in gratitude for his two friends kindness schubert did not die until 1828 after he had written his great ninth symphony forty years later Herbeck a famous conductor obtained the manuscript of the eighth symphony from anselm now an old man by promising to perform one of anselms own overtures its world premiere was in vienna in 1865 and its certain that schubert never heard it performed.

Writing Your Own

1. Listen to a particular piece of music, letting your imagination roam freely as you listen. If possible, hear it twice, and at least one of the times with your eyes closed in complete concentration. Then, at once, make written notes about your thoughts: the pictures, ideas, story or words that came into your mind as you listened. Try then to develop this into a short poem or a piece of very vivid prose writing. Here is an example by a pupil. This one is closely concerned with describing the music itself: you might prefer to describe the day-dreams prompted by it:

A Musical Storm

The piano is whipped up,
Wavelets of viola
Harrass the 'cello,
The kettle-drums boom and vibrate,
A flash of first violin
Tears through the melody;
The storm rises,
The timpani growl menacingly,
Another roll of drum;
The crack of D sharp.
Its energy goes,
And snarling,
He diminishes to pianissimo adagio.

JULIAN

2. What kinds of music do you like, and why? Try to analyse your feelings: is rhythm or melody more important to you? As you listen, do you like to dance or to beat out a rhythm with (say) your fingers, or do you allow your imagination to suggest a whole world of ideas and mental pictures? If vocal music is one of your favourites, how important are the words to you, and does it make much difference if they are in a foreign language? What are your favourite instruments? Think of adjectives or comparisons that would best describe them when played really well. Who are your favourite performers? What has their interpretation got that others lack? Write notes on all these points.

195

Now try to rearrange your rough notes into a complete composition on the subject of:

MY FAVOURITE MUSIC

Arrange the material into paragraphs, so that the reader is led from some general ideas about music and its appeal to your own particular tastes. Include paragraphs on composers and performers, but illustrate throughout from your own experiences: refer to records, concerts, musical programmes on television or radio, and try all the time to show *what* you like about music.

Things To Do

1. Prepare a short talk on *one* musical instrument, anything from a penny whistle to a church organ. You should include an exact description of the instrument (with diagrams that can be pinned up or drawn on the board), and how it produces its range of sounds. If possible, have one with you, and be prepared to play it to illustrate your points. In any case, have some information about the history of the instrument, how it is made, and about some musicians who have used them or been famous for playing them.

Alternatively, make this an illustrated article for the class magazine.

2. A group of the class could make a survey of musical tastes in the class, or the class could undertake a survey of music throughout the school. First, decide on the questions you want to answer: are you simply concerned with a "top ten" of artists or kinds of music, or would you like to investigate how many records people have, or how long they spend listening to music, or whether they play an instrument, or whether they would like more music to be taught at school, and so on? Next, decide on methods: a questionnaire or personal interviews? Finally, make sure that the information will come back in a form that can be assessed and used in a written account: decide whether results should be shown as percentages, etc.

An interesting variation of this would be to interview a number of members of staff about their attitudes to music and music teaching in school.

Books To Read

She Shall Have Music by KITTY BARNE (Dent)
Karen's family are not particularly musical, and it is only after some disappointing setbacks that she finds a really good teacher and works her way up to win a scholarship to a London college of music.

A Swarm in May by WILLIAM MAYNE (O.U.P.)
John Owen, youngest chorister at the Cathedral Choir School, refuses to carry on tradition by acting as the Cathedral's bee-keeper, thinking he dislikes bees. But in helping the organist with his swarm, he discovers quite the opposite, and also makes other exciting discoveries among the Cathedral towers.

The Lark in the Morn by ELFRIDA VIPONT (O.U.P.)
Kit Haverard, youngest of a musical family, discovers when staying with relations after an illness, that she has real musical talent and can sing. With her friends she goes to boarding school and through the ups and downs of musical training. Her story is continued in *The Lark on the Wing.*

Music at Pendragon by PAULA HARRIS (Dent)
Four cousins go for the first time to the musical course held every summer at Pendragon School in Cornwall. They make friends among the varied students and in the many singing and orchestral groups, organized and unofficial, and there are several surprises before the fortnight is over.

The Great Composers series (published by Faber) includes *Bach, Britten, Byrd* and *Holst* (by IMOGEN HOLST), *Beethoven* and *Handel* (by STANLEY SADIE) and *Elgar, Mendelssohn* and *Vaughan Williams* (by MICHAEL HURD). These are fascinating biographies, full also of information and commentary on the works of these masters. (Classified as 780.92)

Instruments of Popular Music, Processional Music, etc. by LILLA M. FOX (Lutterworth)
This series of clear, lively, well-illustrated books forms a comprehensive survey of past and present musical instruments, interesting even to non-musicians. (Classified as 786).

Burt and his friends have followed the course of a disused canal that once served some calamine mines, but only Burt wants to go on and explore the canal tunnel, the mine and the limestone caves. Leaving the others at the entrance, he finds an underground loading wharf, but a pile of fallen stones seems to prevent him from going any further . . .

CHAPTER FIFTEEN

Underground

During the past few minutes he had become aware of the sound of dripping water coming from somewhere above him. It puzzled him. There was nothing to be seen in the roof immediately above where he stood, and yet the sound was close. He raised his torch above his head once more. The light went out. Shaking it, he tried again. This time the light found the hollow above the roof-fall, but it had no centre. There was a hole right through into what looked like another gallery above. Telling himself that this was what it must be, Burt thought he might try to climb up the fallen stones into it. "Just for a look," he told himself. It was close on four o'clock, and the others at the tunnel mouth wouldn't want to be kept waiting about after the real darkness fell.

"Wait till I tell 'em," he gasped out, clambering up the loose rock. It was a good ladder, and it took him to within four feet or so of the hole above him. A moment later he had heaved himself up into it and was standing looking down. Then he flashed his light in an arc around him.

For a moment he wondered if he were really awake. It seemed to him that he was in the very middle of a forest—a forest of pale stone. Everywhere he looked in the light sliced from the dark by his torch there were columns, built down from the roof, and up from the floor, through weary years of dripping water. Those years of dripping water with their burden of limestone sediment were held in stone before him. Seemingly numberless columns stretched in all directions around him and for the first time he felt frightened.

But he also didn't want to go back. Not until he had

explored a little more. He could still hear that sound of dripping water, and he wanted to find where it came from. It was not long before he had found the answer. It came from a tiny stream, falling over a thrust of stone above him in a sparkling curtain; ruched and twisted, the curtain fell into a spangled bowl, along with the stream that had made it, shining like silver in the light of his torch.

Now he wanted to move off into the limestone forest. Yet he hesitated. The hole at his feet was important. If he lost it, he might not find it again, he might even stumble down it in the dark. Eventually he decided to start along one of the twisting paths, leaving a trail of paper to tell him the way back. He would tear the blue wrapper of his chocolate paper to make a trail. He sat down to do the job more comfortably, with his torch between his arched knees.

It was then that Burt heard a noise that sent a chill of fear through him. At first, a rattle of falling rock on rock, then another, then another, larger this time, and then a roar. It was a roar of sliding, crushing rock, coming from below him, under the floor. Then silence. A terrible silence in the darkness all around him. Though he denied it to himself for the next few minutes, he knew already what had happened. Somewhere below him, in the lower gallery, the roof had fallen in. He might be shut in. Trapped in the heart of the fell.

(from Wintercut by Elizabeth Grove)

For Discussion

1. Why did the miners tunnel the canal into the hillside?
2. How did the rock-fall make a good ladder, do you think?
3. What was frightening about the "seemingly numberless columns"?
4. How does dripping water come to form solid columns? What are the technical names for these (a) when built up from the ground, and (b) when growing down from the roof?
5. Was the trail of paper a good idea? How could this plan have gone wrong?
6. "He might be shut in". Why was there some doubt about it?
7. Why was the silence particularly terrible after the fall?
8. Is there anything in this passage to suggest that this happened in winter rather than in summer?
9. What do the following mean?

in an arc	a spangled bowl
sliced from the dark	his arched knees
sediment	a chill of fear
a thrust of stone	the fell
ruched	

10. Was Burt foolish to venture into the tunnel at all?
11. Why should Burt have realised that a rock-fall might cut off his way back?
12. What precautions should cave-explorers (or "pot-holers") take before exploring underground?

For Written Answers

1. Why does the author refer to "the *real* darkness"?
2. Explain in your own words why the sound of dripping water puzzled him.
3. Why did the stone columns seem like a forest?
4. Explain in your own words how these stone columns are made by dripping water.
5. Put in your own words: "Though he denied it to himself for the next few minutes, he knew already what had happened."

God, we don't like to complain —
WE know that the mine is no lark —
But — there's the pools from the rain;
But — there's the cold and the dark.

God, You don't know what it is —
You in Your well-lighted sky,
Watching the meteors whizz;
Warm, with the sun always by.

God, if You had but the moon
Stuck in Your cap for a lamp,
Even You'd tire of it soon,
Down in the dark and the damp.

Nothing but blackness above,
And nothing that moves but the cars —
God, if You wish for our love
Fling us a handful of stars.

LOUIS UNTERMEYER

Discussing The Poem

1. Find out who Caliban was (in Shakespeare's play *The Tempest*), and try to explain the title of this poem.
2. What features of working in a mine does the poem describe? What, for instance, are "the cars"?
3. Why are the miners addressing God? Is the poem suggesting that life in a mine is "God-forsaken"?

Method Exercises

Look carefully at the paragraphing of the passage from *Wintercut*. What is each paragraph about and why did the author go on to a new paragraph in each case? Discuss also the way in which each paragraph is linked to the next. A paragraph is, of course, a series of sentences about one subject or one aspect of a subject, but a good writer ensures that each paragraph leads logically on to the next. Thus, at the end of the first paragraph, the mention of the tempting hole above the fall of stones, and of the others waiting at the tunnel mouth, leads on to the beginning of the next paragraph where he is clambering up and thinking about telling the others what he discovered. Examine the other paragraphs to show how one is linked to the next in each case.

Exercise 1. (a) The following account should be divided into five paragraphs. Indicate where you would divide the passage by writing down the first three and last three words of each paragraph. Be prepared to discuss your reasons for these divisions.

Caves were used as shelters or homes from the earliest times, but for Old Stone Age man many caves seem to have had a further importance. In these caves we find the most remarkable evidence of their skill with painting and sculpture. And the caves containing this evidence are often long distances into the hillside, where there is no daylight and no easy access. Clearly they were not caves to be lived in. On the walls of these caves the primitive artists scratched or painted pictures of the animals they knew and hunted. But they were not painting for the pleasure of decorating the walls. The animals are often shown with arrows piercing them, and it is quite clear that the artists believed that by painting them they were gaining power over them, so that the animals would really appear to be hunted, killed and eaten. This helps explain the great care the artists took to record the animals they hunted, the bulls, horses, deer, reindeer and buffalo. Artists must have worked by the flickering light of torches made of branches or the feeble flames of rough stone lamps burning animal fat. The caves, then, deep in the heart of the hills, were temples for the magic ceremonies of the hunters, and the artists were in the first place magicians seeking power over their prey.

(b) Give each of the five paragraphs a title, summing up what it is really about. Then decide which of the following would be the most suitable title for the *whole* passage.

Caves
Exploring Caves
How Stone Age Man Lived
Stone Age Cave Dwellers
The Artist at Work
Stone Age Cave Paintings
Men and Magic

When, in the passage from *Wintercut*, the author says "the light found the hollow above the roof-fall", he is not using the word "found" literally. "Light" cannot "find" things. A comparison is implied here: the beam of light is like a searcher looking for something. When he talks of a "forest of pale stone", he is again making a comparison, this time between trees in a forest and stone pillars in the cave, rising and arching over Burt's head. These *implied* comparisons are called METAPHORS. They are of course very like *similes*; look at this sentence (adapted from the passage):

The curtain of water fell into a spangled bowl,
shining like silver in the light of his torch.

Here water "shining like silver" is a simile, the word "like" makes it clear that the water is not made of silver. But the "curtain of water" is a metaphor, because in this case the water is treated as if it *is* a curtain. A metaphor is thus a *compressed comparison*, in which one thing is treated as if it *is* another, to which it is being compared.

Exercise 2. What is compared to what in these metaphors and similes? Which are metaphors and which similes?
(a) He saw the stone columns in the light *sliced from the dark by his torch*.
(b) Years of dripping water were *held in stone* before him.
(c) He wanted to move off into *the limestone forests*.

(d) *Like a bee gathering honey* she turned over the leaves of the music.

(e) Under the canopy Karen's hands had *to creep and crawl, finding their way* to the right notes by themselves.

(f) The river *squeezed past* great boulders.

(g) Some of the boulders were *as high as houses*.

(h) We *heard the miniature thunder* where the colt fled.

(i) He shudders his coat *as if to throw off flies*.

(j) The waterfall *arched gracefully* over the brink of the cliff.

Exercise 3. Make up sentences with interesting and original comparisons (similes *or* metaphors) to describe the following:

(a) A large, noisy and impressive waterfall.

(b) A tiny stream in a quiet valley.

(c) A great crane at work on a building site.

(d) A combine harvester at work.

(e) A ballet dancer.

(f) A train emerging from a tunnel.

(g) A still, quiet, warm evening.

(h) Silence returning after a burst of noise.

(i) Tall trees moving in the wind.

(j) Great, white cumulus clouds.

Exercise 4. We referred in Chapter 12 to *phrasal verbs* (e.g. give in, get up, put off). Sometimes the same two words can be switched round and put together to make another (single) verb:

    e.g. look over (= inspect)—overlook (= ignore, superintend, etc.)

In the following sentences, (a) pick out the phrasal verb, (b) write down the single verb that could be made by putting the two words together, and (c) make up a sentence using that single verb (in any appropriate tense):

    e.g. The knights rode proudly out through the castle gate.

    rode out—to outride.

    My horse could easily outride yours.

i. My former friend passed by, pretending not to see me.
ii. The young people took the club over to run it their way.
iii. We saw the swimmer go under for the third time.
iv. They want to turn the factory over to making cars.
v. Set all the skittles up again.
vi. The fourth batsman was run out.
vii. We do not hold with such illegal practices.
viii. She had to pay over all the money in the till to the customer.
ix. The chairman rapidly ran over the points the speakers had made.
x. He threw all his friends over, one by one.

Exercise 5. Look at the following sentences from the passage from *Wintercut*:

> *Shaking* it, he tried again.
> *Telling* himself this was what it might be, Burt thought he might try to climb up the fallen stones to it.
> "Wait till I tell 'em", he gasped out, *clambering* up the loose rock.
> The curtain fell in a spangled bowl, along with the stream that had made it, *shining* like silver in the light of his torch.
> Eventually he decided to start along one of the twisting paths, *leaving* a trail of paper to tell him the way back.

What is the name for the words ending in -ing that have been put in italics? (See Chapter Thirteen if you do not remember.) Here they are acting as adjectives—what does each describe?

The first sentence might have been written:

> He shook it and then he tried again.

Is the version using a present participle an improvement on this?

(a) Rewrite all the other sentences in an alternative (and simpler) form, using the first, as given above, as an example.

(b) Rewrite the following sentences, joining the two parts by using a present participle.

> e.g. He did not have enough money and so he could not go to the cricket match.
>
> Not having enough money, he could not go to the cricket match.

i. He left the others at the entrance and he found an underground loading wharf.
ii. She signalled madly and swept down the slope.
iii. There were several bowls of roses and they were filling the room with a soft perfume.
iv. We found him and he was mowing the grass for his father.
v. The caretaker reminded himself that there are no such things as ghosts, and slowly opened the door of the darkened class-room.
vi. She left a brief note explaining where she had gone and hurried out of the house.
vii. "Come out of there at once!" he cried and beat loudly on the door with his fists.
viii. They had no hope of success and returned dispiritedly.
ix. She returned across the moor alone and felt very lonely and frightened
x. A new bridge had been built so the ferry was closed.

Writing Your Own

Write a dramatic story, involving an escape or people being trapped, or make up your own ending to the story from *Wintercut*. Whichever subject you choose, it is important to remember as vividly as you can what it *feels* like to be in a tight corner. Spend a few minutes recapturing these feelings in your imagination and making notes.

Pay careful attention to planning this story in paragraphs, leading up to a climax. But in any case, make sure that the details are consistent and convincingly *real*.

1. If you, as an individual or as a class, have a chance to visit a mine or any underground caves (officially and in safety, of course,) then take it. Accounts of such a visit, or poems about the world underground, should make excellent material for the class magazine, or a folder or a wall-display.

2. Take one of the following as a topic for library research: use the reference books and books in the sections whose numbers are given.

Coal-mining—in the 18th and 19th centuries (942.07). Coal-mining—today (622.33). Salt-mining (664.4). Copper-mining or tin-mining (622.33). Tunnelling—the 18th and 19th century pioneers (942). Tunnelling today (624.19). The geography of canals in Britain (386). Canal building (627, 386). Some famous canals (386). The modern restoration of canals. Canal boats, past and present (623). Caving and pot-holing as a pastime (551.44). Great natural caves (551.44). Cave-men (571). Cave-paintings (709). Beautiful caves and rock-formations (551.44). How coal has been formed, and why it burns (622). Smelting iron ore (672). Mining rare minerals. Tapping underground supplies of oil (665). Tapping underground supplies of natural gas (665). Oil refining (665). Careers in mining (371.425).

3. In connection with topics in question 2, write business letters to the following organizations, asking for information and free pamphlets. (Only *one* letter should be sent to each address, on behalf of the class.)

> The Public Relations Department,
>> The National Coal Board,
>>> Hobart House,
>>>> Grosvenor Place,
>>>>> London SW1X 7AE.

Shell Education Service,
Shell International Petroleum Co. Ltd.,
Shell Centre,
London SE1 7NA.

The Public Relations Officer,
British Waterways Board,
Melbury House,
Melbury Terrace,
London NW1 6JX.

Books To Read

Wintercut by ELIZABETH GROVE (White Lion)
In this realistic story of canal life, Joe and Sal, young people born and bred on the narrow boats, find themselves spending a week ashore with Don and his cousin Burt, while their boat is laid up. They find plenty of interest and excitement prospecting the possible course for a new canal, as well as exploring the disused cut to the old mines.

The Cave by RICHARD CHURCH (Heinemann; Pan)
The five boys of the Tomahawk Club secretly plan an expedition to explore a cave near their home on the River Severn. This tremendously exciting adventure becomes dangerous and is a stern test of endurance for each member of the gang. In *Down River* (Heinemann) the Club continues the investigation the following summer, against sinister opposition.

They Found a Cave by NAN CHAUNCY (O.U.P.)
A group of children try making their home, temporarily, in a cave in a Tasmanian hillside; the continued lack of comfort puts their one rule—that they won't grumble—very severely to the test, but they refuse to give up their exile until their aunt returns from hospital.

Caving by JAMES LOVELOCK (Batsford)
Caving is an exciting but dangerous and demanding sport, not to be undertaken alone, or without preparation and training. Here is a clear, well-informed book by an experienced caver to give an insight into the fascination and the techniques of an increasingly popular pastime. (Classified as 796.5)

Emma, who has always been colour blind, takes three mysterious pills which are supposed to give her colour vision. After taking the last one she faints and shortly after recovering consciousness she realises something is different . . . .

CHAPTER SIXTEEN

To Sharpen Your Senses

She clenched her fists, remaining very still; but her heart raced as she thought, "It's happened! It's happened! Oh God! Thank you! it's happened!" And yet was it possible? Could such a thing happen?

Emma opened her right eye just a fraction, so that she could see between her eyelashes, and it *was* true. There was the green of grass sown with buttercups and dandelions like brass buttons, and the white petals and yellow centres of daisies.

A sudden chill of fear struck her and she closed her eyes again. This was very, very dangerous. She had read descriptions of colour, in books, and people had told her what things looked like in colour, but none of them had conveyed to her even the tiniest fraction of what she had already seen was the most miraculous and beautiful thing in the whole world, the infinitely varied glory of colour. There was not one green but tens of thousands of different shades of green; and when they said grass was green, it was also yellow and brown and nearly black in places, and in others nearly white.

Perhaps people who had seen colour all their lives had never noticed that, or had just grown lazy about looking, calling grass green because it was more green than it was any other colour. And then she would be tempted to tell them that they had never really looked at colour, and they would say, "How do you know?" They would laugh and say, "You're colour-blind and yet you pretend to know." And then she would be tempted to say what had happened . . . .

She opened her eyes again as she heard a crack and a burst of applause. The red ball bounded towards her across the grass, a white-clad, sweating shiny-black-haired man pounding behind it. He flung his arm up as it crossed the boundary. The inside of the arm was pink and smooth, the outside covered with golden hairs, the skin red-brown underneath. He flung the ball to the bowler as the batsmen walked back to their wickets.

The sky was not one but a dozen shades of blue varying in depth. Where there was thick white woolly cloud, the blue of the sky round was darker than at the edges of thin feathery clouds. That means, Emma thought, a colour is not its colour all by itself, but what it's next to changes it. She saw that the sun on the top of the roof of the cottage silhouetted against the sky made a line of light between the red roof and the grey of the cloud beyond . . . .

Then she remembered that Druce the chemist had a weighing-machine in the entrance to his shop, and in the centre of its face she thought there was a mirror. Druce's was in the middle of the village, but she ran there and reached it out of breath. The moment she saw that there was a mirror, she stopped running.

She walked slowly up to it, approaching it from the side. Then gingerly she peered round at her reflection.

Her heart sank.

Of course she had been running and it was hot. That explained the great red flush at her neck and under her chin. But those rusty great freckles on her nose and cheeks, those great thick almost white eyelashes like a cow's! And worst of all, the nakedness of her face! She had never seen a face as terribly open as hers. It was like looking into a brightly-lit room and being able to see everything that was happening because no blinds or curtains had been drawn. "Oh, dear! Oh, dear!" she thought. "I'll have to wear a veil!"

(from *The Fair to Middling* by Arthur Calder-Marshall)

For Discussion

1. How did Emma explain the fact that people with ordinary colour-vision find colours less exciting than she did? Do you agree with her theory and explanation?
2. What does "varying in depth" mean when applied to blue?
3. Can you give other examples of adjacent colours influencing one another, as when the blue of the sky looked darker at the edges of the thicker clouds?
4. Why did Emma slow down when she got to Druce's entrance and sidle up to the weighing machine?
5. Why was she so shocked at seeing her face in the mirror? Do you find this part of the story convincing?
6. Are any members of the class colour-blind? Would most colour-blind people have this kind of shock if they were suddenly able to see all colours?
7. Do you think colour-blindness is a disadvantage in modern life? If so, why, and in what circumstances?
8. Emma found grass to be many different colours; what can alter the normal colour of grass?
   Can you give examples of (a) water not looking blue, (b) slate roofs not looking grey, or (c) other misleading generalisations about colour (e.g. that European people's skins are "white")?

For Written Answers

1. Where was Emma when she took the third pill and fainted?
2. Bearing in mind that Emma had promised not to tell anyone about the three magic pills, explain why it was so "dangerous" that she found colours exciting.
3. Why did Emma hurry to Druce's shop?
4. Explain in your own words, with examples of your own, what Emma means by a colour not being a "colour all by itself".
5. Explain (again in your own words and with examples) what Emma means by the "infinitely varied glory of colour".

213

Smells

Why is it that the poets tell
So little of the sense of smell?
These are the odours I love well:

The smell of coffee freshly ground;
Or rich plum pudding, holly crowned;
Or onions fried and deeply browned.

The fragrance of a fumy pipe;
The smell of apples newly ripe;
And printers' ink on leaden type.

Woods by moonlight in September
Breathe most sweet; and I remember
Many a smoky camp-fire ember.

Camphor, turpentine, and tea,
The balsam of a Christmas tree,
These are whiffs of gramarye . . . .
A ship smells best of all to me!

CHRISTOPHER MORLEY

Discussing The Poem

1. Is it true that there are few poems about (or mentioning) smells? Can you think of any at all?
2. Do you agree with Christopher Morley's choice of well-loved smells? What would you add or take away?
3. What does "whiffs of gramarye" mean? Why is the last line in italics? Is there any other difference between the last verse and the first four?

As we saw in Chapter Ten, some verbs have objects, as in:

Emma opened her right *eye*.

Others have complements; adjectives, as in:

Emma had always been *colour-blind*.

or nouns, as in:

The glory of colour was the most beautiful *thing* in the whole world.

But a number of verbs do not take objects or complements:

She faints. Her heart raced. It has happened.

Emma cannot "faint" anything—these are verbs that are complete in themselves. Of course, adverbs can be added:

People would laugh.

One cannot laugh anything; but people might laugh *loudly* or *immediately* or *at Emma*. All these would be adverbs or adverb phrases, saying how, when or where people would laugh.

Verbs that require objects are called TRANSITIVE (literally meaning: "going across"—the sense goes across from verb to object). Verbs that do not require objects (or complements) to make sense are called INTRANSITIVE. Dictionaries often label verbs *v.t.* (or *trans.*) and *v.i.*—find some examples of these in a dictionary. Some verbs can be *both*, in different senses:

Transitive: Emma read the instructions.

Intransitive: Emma was always reading.

Exercise 1. (a) Write out the verbs (in full) from the following sentences, and state whether each is transitive or intransitive. If it is transitive, state what the object word is.

  i. She clenched her fists.

  ii. Could such a thing happen?

  iii. A sudden chill of fear struck her.

  iv. She had read descriptions of colour in books.

  v. She heard a crack and a burst of applause.

  vi. The red ball bounded towards her.

  vii. He flung his arm up.

  viii. The batsmen walked back to their wickets.

  ix. She ran quickly there.

  x. She reached the shop out of breath.

(b) Make up short sentences using each of the following verbs (i.) transitively, with an object, and (ii.) intransitively, without an object.

> e.g. ride (i.) He rode his bicycle home.
> (ii.) He rode very well.

| fight | return | turn | run | sweep |
| cover | leave | play | slide | cook |

Exercise 2. Many verbs can be transitive or intransitive, but in a few cases English has two similar verbs, one transitive, the other intransitive. For example:

> To lie (intransitive) = to be in a horizontal position.
> To lay (transitive) = to put (something) down.

Other examples are to fall (intrans.), to fell (trans.) and to rise (intrans.), to raise (trans.)

"Lie" is particularly confusing, because its past tense is "lay", and because there is a third verb, "to lie" (intrans.) = to tell an untruth. Here are the various forms of these three verbs: which is which?

> He lies, he lied, he is lying, he has lied.
> He lies, he lay, he is lying, he has lain.
> He lays, he laid, he is laying, he has laid.

Rewrite the following sentences, choosing the correct form of lie, lay, etc. to fill each of the gaps (only *one* word is required for each gap).

(a) I —— awake most of last night.
(b) Mother asked me to —— the table.
(c) He cackled as if he had just —— an egg.
(d) He —— to us then when he said he was —— in the bushes listening to the smugglers.
(e) The grass where the oak beam had —— was flattened and discoloured.
(f) Mother was —— down, trying to rest.
(g) The professor —— the specimen down carefully on the sheet of glass.
(h) —— that parcel down for minute, John.
(i) Our horse was then —— fourth in the race.

Exercise 3. As we saw in Book One, tenses of verbs are often a source of confusion in English. Rewrite the following sentences in the *past tense*, using a dictionary to check the correct form.

 e.g. The waves break relentlessly on the shore.
    The waves broke relentlessly on the shore.

(a) She easily becomes jealous.
(b) The gale blows itself out.
(c) Their dog drinks water.
(d) The sun shines brightly on the water.
(e) I ring my friend up every Sunday.
(f) They run a club for spastic children.
(g) She swims beautifully.
(h) The old blacksmith shoes horses for the nearby stables.
(i) In autumn, trees shed their leaves.
(j) This loom weaves cloth faster than the others.
(k) Slow and steady wins the race.
(l) He always throws a party at Christmas.
(m) My father winds up the kitchen clock every Saturday night.
(n) The tiger springs on its prey.
(o) Nettles sting him all over.

Exercise 4. (a) Find out what the following adjectives mean; then rearrange them in eight groups of three, so that in each group there are three *synonyms* to describe tastes or smells.

acid	fragrant	piquant	salt	sweet
aromatic	hot	putrid	sharp	tart
balmy	insipid	rancid	sour	tasteless
briny	mordant	rank	spicy	vapid
candied	peppery	saline	sugary	

(b) Try to describe the following colours—perhaps in terms of a mixture of other colours.

e.g. Peacock blue is a strong greenish blue, as found in a peacock's tail feathers.

scarlet	olive green	yellow ochre	buff	red ochre
crimson	cobalt	tangerine	purple	charcoal grey
pink	turquoise	cream	mauve	indigo

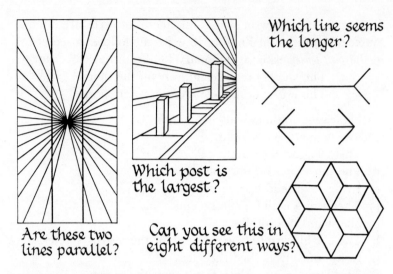

Which line seems the longer?

Which post is the largest?

Are these two lines parallel?

Can you see this in eight different ways?

Exercise 5. Rewrite the following conversation about optical illusions, putting in all the punctuation necessary, including capital letters and apostrophes. The arrangement in paragraphs has been correctly set out for you. Two of the paragraphs are comment, and are not spoken by John or his uncle.

ill believe it when i see it said john angrily

you think you can trust your own eyes then asked uncle bob

of course i can exclaimed john

uncle bob took a pencil and ruled two lines in the shape of an inverted T

which is longer he asked

john looked carefully the vertical one he said firmly

no replied his uncle taking the ruler and measuring them they are exactly the same length pass me that pair of compasses

he then drew two circles each 10 mm in diameter and began to draw a series of larger circles round one of them and a series of smaller circles round the other

you see he said triumphantly the 10 mm circles look different the way we see things is altered by their surroundings and we cannot always trust our own eyes

Because Emma was seeing colours literally for the first time, she noticed details that would have been taken for granted by most people. When writers describe things, places, people or events, it is part of their job to see them freshly, to look again at what the rest of us take for granted, and describe the experiences so that the reader sees and thinks about them afresh, or sees new truths about them. Here are suggestions for compositions in which you could practise looking at things afresh:

(a) Shut your eyes for some time and think hard about what it must be like to be totally blind. Imagine that you have been blind for some time or from birth. A miraculous operation has restored your sight. Describe the moment when the nurse removes the bandages and you *see* for the first time.

(b) Imagine that you have been colour blind (or partially colour blind), like Emma, and that, like her, you are given the chance to be cured. Again, describe what you see and feel.

(c) Describe the scenes around you from some unusual angle: from the top of the highest hill or tallest building, or from a semi-basement window, or as seen through coloured glasses.

(d) Imagine that you are an ant, a butterfly, a fish, a skylark, or some tiny creature like the inhabitants of Lilliput in Swift's *Gulliver's Travels*. Describe what you would see and experience. The Lilliputians who were only fifteen centimetres tall made a list of the objects in Gulliver's pockets. Here is an extract; what are they describing?

> There were two pockets which we could not enter: these he called his fobs; they were two large slits cut into the top of his middle cover, but squeezed close by the pressure of his belly. Out of the right fob hung a great silver chain, with a wonderful kind of engine at the bottom. We directed him to draw out whatever was fastened to that chain; which appeared to be a globe, half silver, and half of some transparent metal; for on the transparent side we saw certain strange figures circularly drawn, and thought we could touch them, till we found our fingers stopped by that lucid substance. He put this engine

to our ears, which made an incessant noise like that of a water-mill: and we conjecture it is either some unknown animal, or the god that he worships; but we are more inclined to the latter opinion, because he assures us (if we understood him right, for he expressed himself very imperfectly) that he seldom did anything without consulting it: he called it his oracle, and said it pointed out the time for every action of his life. From the left fob he took out a net almost large enough for a fisherman, but contrived to open and shut like a purse, and served him for the same use: we found therein several massy pieces of yellow metal, which, if they be real gold, must be of immense value.

Things To Do

1. Let members of the class bring to school as many as possible of the following: small mirrors (ordinary, black or coloured, concave, convex or distorting), sun-glasses (various colours), glass balls (coloured or plain), magnifying glasses, telescopes and binoculars, microscopes, coloured vases, coloured or plain bottles, pieces of reeded, patterned or frosted glass, coloured gelatines, kaleidoscopes, periscopes, jars of water. Let these be passed round and thoroughly examined: look through both ends of the telescope, for instance, and through the bottle when held longways and slowly revolved. Each member of the class should then choose one of these objects or one view and begin to describe exactly what he sees. Choose fresh, original and vivid words and comparisons. Write a poem, if you wish.

The best of these descriptions and poems could be included in the next number of the class magazine or written out neatly for display on the board or in a folder.

2. Small groups in the class can prepare some interesting games for the rest to play. One group should sew into small cloth bags dry samples of different well-known domestic substances: sugar, coffee beans, rice, dried peas, pepper corns, cloves, etc. The contents must be guessed by *feeling* alone.

Another group can put on to saucers samples of substances that can be *tasted* by someone when blindfolded: ginger, sugar, curry-powder, pepper, salt, celery salt, mustard powder, sherbet, flour, etc. (Warn the victims not to take too much!)

A third group make up a series of small bottles of liquids that have distinctive *smells* (paraffin, methylated spirit, lighter fuel, vinegar, lemon essence, tomato sauce, etc.)—again to be guessed blindfold.

A fourth group arrange to make common *noises* behind a curtain: striking a match, sharpening a knife, winding a clock, closing a book, tearing cloth, etc.

Books To Read

The Fair to Middling by ARTHUR CALDER-MARSHALL (Hart-Davis; Penguin)
The children of Alderman Winterbottome's School for Incapacitated Orphans each have different, but equally strange, experiences at the Fair. Each of them has the chance to become like an ordinary child, but, curiously, in the end they seem to prefer to be their own incapacitated selves.

Gulliver's Travels by JONATHAN SWIFT (various publishers)
In these classic stories, Gulliver visits a land of tiny people, a land of giants, and other countries where people and customs are strangely unlike our own. Notice how the author was making fun of the stupidity and narrow-mindedness of the Europeans.

The Phantom Tollbooth by NORTON JUSTER (Collins)
What sort of meal would you expect if you had to eat your own words? What happens when you eat subtraction stew? As Milo discovers when he visits Dictionopolis, where words are all-important, and Digitopolis, which is dominated by numbers, there is something to be said for the Wisdom of the Princesses Rhyme and Reason.

Marianne Dreams by CATHERINE STORR (Penguin)
The story of a girl, kept in bed by illness, who finds a pencil with magic properties and begins a dream-relationship with Mark, who is also ill. Through Marianne's drawings they share a weird adventure, besieged in a bleak house on a moor by one-eyed stones, until Marianne learns to control the terror with her pencil.

Sandra meets Mike by chance, when they both join in an archaeological "dig" on the Maythorn Hills. She invites him back to tea and finds that her grandmother, Mrs. Leigh, does not altogether approve of her choice of a friend. Before tea Mike and Sandra go upstairs to wash their hands.

CHAPTER SEVENTEEN

Out To Tea

She led the way down. She stopped short on the threshold of one room, and backed out again as though surprised. He had just time to see, over her shoulder, a pale blue room with a big dining-table and nothing on it except a bowl of roses. "Where are we having tea, Gran?" she called.

"Where do you expect, darling?" came Mrs. Leigh's voice from near-by. "Isn't it usual to have tea in the drawing-room?"

They went into the next room. Mrs. Leigh was sitting at a trolley-table with the cups and saucers in front of her.

"I just thought we'd be sitting up," Sandra apologised. "I mean, we do sometimes use the dining-room when it isn't grown-ups, and ——"

"But, darling, I thought you were so insistent that you *are* grown up—or nearly?" Mrs. Leigh's expression was mild and innocent, as if her one object in life was to please her grand-daughter. But Mike had his doubts. "Do sit down, Michael," she told him.

"Thanks, Mrs. Leigh."

He subsided into the nearest arm-chair and wished he had chosen a smaller one. Subside was the word. It was so deep and soft it engulfed him like a swamp. He wondered desperately how he would ever get out of it again. Meanwhile, how was he going to manage his cup and saucer, the little plate and the finicky little tea-knife and the various good things which were being offered him? . . . .

It wasn't only the eating and drinking that were awkward. It was the talk.

Mrs. Leigh kept asking questions. She was ever so polite—
you couldn't say she was rude—but the general effect was
snooty. It was as though she had just turned over a stone, and
found Mike underneath it, and wasn't too pleased with what
she saw.

She made him feel that even the way he talked was wrong.
Not just his accent, but the words he used.

"Your teacher?" she would echo him. "Oh, I see—a *schoolmaster*."

"No, Mrs. Leigh, it's a lady."

"Oh, really? And tell me, do you like being taught by a
woman?"

"She's not bad."

"I'm very glad to hear *that*."

I suppose (Mike said to himself) that's what people mean
when they talk about "gentle" sarcasm. He didn't like sarcasm
of any kind.

He ought never to have come, he thought miserably. The
idea of tea at Sandra's place had sounded all right, but he
wasn't really having tea with Sandra, he was having tea with
Sandra's grandmother. Sandra wasn't saying much, though she
was looking pretty mad when Mike glanced in her direction.
She must have spotted what her gran was up to.

"So you don't learn Latin at your school? Dear me, I don't
think I have ever met a schoolboy who didn't have to learn
Latin. Won't you find it a great handicap if you ever want to
go to the University? But no, I suppose you won't be going . . .
Though one never knows these days. With all these grants and
scholarships I suppose there is no reason why anyone shouldn't
go to the University." . . .

Mike was heartily thankful when the clock struck five and
(though he knew it was only a few minutes' walk to the
station) he could start saying it was time to go.

"Must you really? I expect you'd like to wash your hands
again—honey is such terrible stuff, isn't it?" She smiled, She
couldn't have looked nicer or more friendly. "Well, you know
your way up, Michael."

"Thanks very much, Mrs. Leigh. Won't be a sec.," he muttered to Sandra.

He got himself out of the room and upstairs. His hands *were* faintly sticky and the mirror showed a smear which the cream sandwich had left on his lip. Mam might have said the same sort of thing to Rex—made a joke of it, and pushed him out to the scullery to "wipe his whiskers"—but Mam would have done it somehow differently. She wouldn't have made Rex feel small . . . .

(from *The Maythorn Story* by Geoffrey Trease)

For Discussion

1. Why did Mrs. Leigh choose to have tea in the drawing room?

2. What was sarcastic about Mrs. Leigh's "I'm very glad to hear *that*"?

3. Do you agree with Mike in disliking *all* kinds of sarcasm? What is unpleasant about sarcasm?

4. Why was the word "subside" so appropriate?

5. " . . . as if her one object in life was to please her granddaughter." What was her object in conducting the tea-party and the conversation in this way? What did Sandra feel about this?

6. Sandra's surname was Clifford and her grandmother had been careful to see that Mike knew he should call her Mrs. Leigh. How often does he do so? Does this seem deliberate (or unnatural), do you think?

7. How did Mrs. Leigh make Mike feel that he talked badly?

8. What were Mrs. Leigh's ideas about who should go to university? Would you agree with her?

9. What is the contrast between the way Mrs. Leigh and Mike's Mam would have dealt with a guest's sticky fingers and face. Does it tell us anything about the two women?

10. Why are the words "dig", "gentle" and "wipe his whiskers" in inverted commas? Explain the use of italics for various words and phrases in this passage.

11. Discuss what you think are the important things to remember when entertaining guests who feel rather strange and bewildered in your house.

12. Are there *any* occasions when it would be right for someone to make a guest "feel small"?

For Written Answers

1. Which room did they have tea in, and why did this surprise Sandra?

2. What kind of schoolboy do you think Mrs. Leigh had met, up to her meeting with Mike?

3. Did Mike need to go at 5 o'clock? If not, why did he start saying it was time to go?

4. Was Mrs. Leigh really using her "tactics" against Mike, or against Sandra? Give an explanation for your answer.

5. Without referring to the rest of this book, make some deductions about the kind of home Mike came from and the kind of boy he was, from this passage.

Method Exercises

Using a present participle, as in Chapter Fifteen, is not, of course, the only way of joining sentences more interestingly than with "and, but, or, then", etc. Consider this example:

Sandra had met Mike on a "dig" and she took him home to a tea-party but this was not a great success.

This could be written:

Sandra, who had met Mike on a "dig", took him home to a tea-party, which was not a great success.

The pronouns *who, whom, which, that,* and the adjective *whose* can all be used in this way, but there are certain common mistakes to be avoided. As we saw in Chapter Fourteen, "who" is the subject of the verb that follows it, "whom" is the object, and these two are often confused.

A good way to remember this correctly is to think of "who" as equivalent to "he" and "whom" as equivalent to "him", as in these sentences:

Sandra met a young man *and he* was very friendly.

Sandra met a young man *who* was very friendly.

Sandra met a young man *and* her grandmother did not like *him*.

Sandra met a young man *whom* her grandmother did not like.

Secondly, *who, whom* refer to people, *which* refers to things:

A person who . . . . A bicycle which . . . .

Thirdly, *that* can refer to persons *or* things, and be subject or object, but it must not be confused with *what:*

He is the kind of person *that* you can respect.

(Not "what you can respect.")

Fourthly, *whose* (= of whom, of which) is easily confused with *who's* (= who is, who has).

Exercise 1. Join the two parts of each of the following, replacing the words in italics by "who, whom, that, which" or "whose", and making any other necessary changes, as in the examples above.

(a) Mike bought a lot of cakes *and they* were by no means all sticky.

(b) The assistant has gone off duty *and he* served you.

(c) Pegasus was a horse *and it* was supposed to have wings.

(d) The old lady has moved *and* you used to run errands for *her*.

(e) *Sandra's* parents were abroad *and so* Sandra lived with her grandmother.

(f) Is this the bicycle? Was *this bicycle* stolen?

(g) The thieves stole several items from the store *and they* were never caught.

(h) The thieves stole several items from the store *and they* were never recovered.

(i) The thieves stole several items from the store *and it* was closed for the day.

(j) This is the manager *and his* store was robbed.

Exercise 2. Rewrite the following sentences, correcting the mistakes in them:

(a) Those tickets what you gave me were forgeries.

(b) The youth who we saw outside number 19 was later arrested.

(c) Who is that? The man whose won the competition.

(d) George is the candidate whom, we hope, will be elected chairman of the club.

(e) The candidate which gets two thirds of the votes is elected.

(f) Can you think of anyone in the class who's work is more impressive?

(g) I heard what you said and I found the papers what you asked for.

(h) A man whose lost everything and whose house has been destroyed obviously needs help.

(i) Who's hat is this? Does it belong to anyone that we know?

(j) We asked her what she had done with the money what she had earned.

Exercise 3. In Book One we saw that many nouns and pronouns could be varied in number, gender and person.

(a) Write the noun or pronoun of feminine gender that corresponds to each of the following masculine nouns or pronouns.

e.g., prince—princess

wizard	bull	colt	son-in-law
marquis	peacock	buck	nephew
duke	fox	stag	stallion
heir	him	bachelor	dog
ram	drake	bridegroom	himself

(b) Write the plural forms of the following nouns or pronouns:

e.g., tomato—tomatoes

brother-in-law	mine(noun)	handkerchief	jockey
man-of-war	pretence	handful	fly
its	apprentice	fantasy	lass
himself	transparency	octopus	reindeer
mine(pronoun)	radio	memento	mongoose

228

(c) Give the second person pronouns corresponding to these first person pronouns:

e.g., we—you

I   us   ours   myself   ourselves

Exercise 4. In all of the following sentences *except one,* there is a lack of "agreement" between subject and verb, or elsewhere in the sentence; for instance, in some there is a change from plural to singular:

They was quite sure they was right.

which should be either:

"They were . . . " or "He was . . . "

Correct the following wherever necessary. (But do NOT alter the tenses.)

(a) There was plenty of opportunities for promotion.

(b) I was going to give ourselves a treat.

(c) Half a kilo of tomatoes were being sold for thirty pence.

(d) Each of the guests at the party had their own pads and pencils.

(e) Give John and I a chance, and we shall succeed.

(f) She were a real beauty, that boat was!

(g) Let each of us return to his own house for the night.

(h) He and she then find herself in a very clean and richly furnished room.

(i) There are not one man in thousands who know that secret.

(j) Of the two milk bottles, neither were empty and one was full to the top.

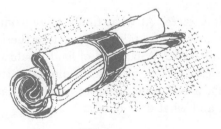

Exercise 5. Sandra invited Mike to tea quite informally, without a written invitation. If she had been arranging a larger party (perhaps for a birthday) she would probably have used a written invitation card and expected a written reply, so that she would know how many guests to prepare for. Invitation cards can be bought to suit all occasions, but it is often more friendly and personal to make your own.

(a) Very formal invitations are traditionally in the third person (as if both host and guest were acting through a secretary!):

Lady Amelia Jones
requests the pleasure of the company of
John Fortescue
at a soirée at her home
on Friday, August 10th, 19—
at 8 o'clock.

R.S.V.P. to
The Glade,
Botsworth,   *Dress*
Hants,   *optional*
SO12 8PL

The answer has to be in the third person:

John Fortescue
has great pleasure in accepting
Lady Amelia Jones's kind invitation
to her soirée on 10th August.

What is a soirée? At what time of day would you expect to go to one, or to a cocktail party, or to a sherry party, or to a wedding breakfast? What kind of food would you expect to be offered to eat at each of these: a dinner party, a cheese and wine party, a barbecue, a buffet lunch? What does R.S.V.P. stand for, and what does it mean?

(b) For most of us, most of the time, less formal (and more friendly) invitations are more appropriate. Here is the kind of letter Sandra might have written to Mike to invite him to a birthday party, if Mrs. Leigh had not disapproved of him so much. Notice that she includes the time the party will end— perhaps her grandmother made her do this because she had visions of a noisy teenage party going on all night. Anyway, it will help Mike when it comes to looking up trains home.

Apple Garth,
Beacon Lane,
LITTLE MAYTHORN,
Westershire.
1st July, 19—.

Dear Mike,

We are having a small party here on Saturday, July 16th, from 4.0 o'clock until about 9.00 p.m., to celebrate my birthday, and I very much hope you will be able to come.

Most of the boys and girls you met up on the Beacon when you were last here will be coming, and we are looking forward to seeing you again.

Yours sincerely,
Sandra

P.S. Let me know if you can come.

Write Mike's reply, either accepting or refusing this invitation. Pay careful attention to the correct setting out and punctuation of his address (17, Alma Road, Ninefields, HAR-BOROUGH) and the date, etc.

Writing Your Own

When Mike returned home, he found it very difficult to tell his family about having tea at "Apple Garth". He realised that he could not even hint about Mrs. Leigh's superior manner without making his parents angry and himself embarrassed. Yet most people have had experiences like that of the tea-party: times when they felt ashamed, embarrassed or inadequate. Try to describe one such experience, whether real or imaginary. Be careful to build up the atmosphere and background with full description, and pay particular attention to the *people* involved. Let their appearances and personalities come out as clearly as Mrs. Leigh's do in this passage. The incident does not have to be connected with visiting or entertaining, of course, so long as it is (or was) embarrassing.

Things To Do

1. Prepare an article for the class magazine or some talks to the class on giving a party to entertain friends of your own age. Groups might divide the subject between them, including:

Inviting the guests—advice on numbers, invitations, balancing the sexes, etc.

Breaking the ice—introductions, games and other devices to help people mix and get to know each other.

Music and dancing—with ideas on novelty dances.

Team games, noisy games; pencil and paper games.

Party magic, acting or charades.

Food and costs.

Unusual ways of serving the food and drink.

Recommended books for party-givers.

2. Find out more about *archaeology*. What is a "dig"? What kinds of places do archaeologists dig in? What are they looking for? Find some illustrations of important archaeological discoveries, and some examples of "finds" in your own area. How do archaeologists date their finds? If you find something of interest, where should you take it, or report it?

Books on archaeology are classified under 913 and 571.

3. An awkward tea-party might be developed as a situation for
for an impromptu play. It should offer scope for very definite
characters: proud, nervous, talkative, shy, angry, sarcastic,
rude, polite. Decide on a basic situation and set of characters
(perhaps using the story of Mike at Sandra's as a starting-point),
and then see how the play can be developed spontaneously.

Books To Read

The Maythorn Story by GEOFFREY TREASE (Heinemann)
Mike's own town world of Harborough and Ninefields, with
the difficult girl Shirley next door, and the derelict "island site"
where he had played for years, later becomes curiously mixed
up with the world of Sandra and the archaeological finds on
the Maythorn Hills.
A Sound of Chariots by MOLLIE HUNTER (Collins)
When Bridie McShane's father dies she becomes especially
conscious of what he stood for, what he meant to her, and what
he and she had in common. This is a moving story about a
young girl growing up in Scotland soon after 1918, and gradually
discovering her talent as a writer.
The Changeling by ZILPHA KEATLEY SNYDER (Lutterworth)
This is a shrewd, entertaining story of two girls growing up in
California: Martha, easily frightened, but from a respectable,
stable home, and her close friend, Ivy, from the notorious
Carson family, always asserting that she is really a changeling,
who does not quite belong in that world.
Introducing Archaeology by MAGNUS MAGNUSSON (Bodley Head)
This is an interesting outline of the history of this study, from
the time of the Babylonian archaeologist, King Naborcidus, to
the modern techniques of radio-carbon dating, by a well-known
enthusiast and expert.
Digging Up the Past by SIR LEONARD WOOLLEY (Benn)
This is a personal and expert account of work by one of the
most famous English archaeologists. (Both books classified as
913.031)

When you visit the seaside, go down to the shallows and rock-pools at low tide. Do you realise just how many curious creatures live on the sand, in the pools, under rocks, in caves and amongst the seaweed?

CHAPTER EIGHTEEN

The Sea-shore

The most exciting place on the sea-shore is a rock-pool, with its glistening gardens of seaweeds and sponges.

Here you will find some of the most striking of all marine creatures and among them will be the sea-anemone—their graceful forms bending and swaying with the ebb and flow of the sea, their tentacles spread out in the water like the petals of a flower.

The Greeks called anemones "Flower animals". It is not surprising that many people are still puzzled as to whether they are plants or animals. But although they may look flower-like, anemones are most decidedly animals, and greedy animals at that. Like many sea animals they prey upon the other small creatures that live around them.

The swaying movements of their arms draw unsuspecting victims within reach and the slightest touch spells death to the creatures on which the anemones feed, for each anemone is a beautiful, but deadly sea-nettle. Shrimps, crabs, worms and small fishes are first paralysed and then consumed. Anemones have been known to seize quite large animals and if they are too large to be digested all at once, they are drawn in slowly by degrees. Later the undigested parts, shell, horny legs, etc., are ejected out of its mouth.

These waving tentacles are studded with thousands of sting-ing cells—each a coiled thread with a sharp dart at the end; each capable of delivering a numbing sting. The moment contact is made the tentacles begin to close round the victim, finally enfolding it completely and drawing it into the anemone's mouth.

235

If the pools are left high and dry when the tide goes out the anemones close down. Their tentacles are withdrawn and tucked away out of sight, and all that is left are coloured blobs of jelly—red, pink or green—gleaming like polished leather.

Even though the hot sun beats down on the blobs they do not dry up, for they are full of water. When the tide swirls in again, filling the rock-pools and renewing the stock of small animal life on which the anemones feed, they again spread out their rings of tentacles, turning the pools into submarine gardens.

Touch them with your finger and they will again close up. Have you ever wondered how an anemone is able to open up and close down at will? When it wants to expand from a mere blob and stretch out its tentacles it does so by pumping itself up with water, drawing it in not only through its mouth but also through the many tiny holes which cover the body wall.

To close down again all it has to do is to squirt out the water rapidly through all its openings and the long tentacles and the feathery plumes are withdrawn from sight.

The anemone fastens itself securely to the rock face by means of a single foot. This is really a strong sucker with which it clings so firmly that it almost seems to be growing out of the rock. Most anemones do not have to spend all their lives in the same place. Sometimes they detach themselves and glide slowly over the surface of the rock, on their base or foot, until they come to a more suitable spot in which to make their home.

Many anemones have a curious way of sending their young out into the world. The female retains the eggs until they are just ready to hatch and then she coughs her entire brood of tiny larvae out of her mouth into the open sea. These little creatures swim about very actively for a time, sometimes drifting long distances with the moving sea. Eventually most of them find suitable rocks on which to settle and grow.

(from *Along the Edge of the Sea* by Jill Norman)

For Discussion

1. Explain "ebb" and "flow" and what causes tides.
2. What is the distinction between a plant and an animal which means that sea-anemones are "decidedly animals"?
3. In what way is a sea-anemone like a nettle?
4. How mobile is a sea-anemone?
5. What would you expect a "suitable spot in which to make their home" to be like?
6. What do sea-anemones feed on? Do they eat *all* their prey?
7. Examine the paragraphing of this passage: what is the main theme of each paragraph and how does each paragraph lead on to the next?
8. What is the singular of "larvae"?
9. Comment on the following similes and metaphors: what is the comparison that each is making?

> tentacles spread out in the water like the petals of a flower
>
> stinging cells—each a coiled thread with a sharp dart at the end
>
> blobs of jelly—red, pink or green—gleaming like polished leather
>
> it does so by pumping itself up with water.

10. What have you found most fascinating and exciting at the sea—fish, shore life, bird-life, rocks and caves, swimming, games on the beach, boat trips, amusement arcades, or what? Try to explain the fascination.

For Written Answers

1. Do anemones kill their prey before consuming them?
2. How would you recognise an anemone (a) under water, (b) when left dry?
3. Why can anemones be said to "turn the pools into submarine gardens"?
4. Explain in your own words: (a) how anemones catch their prey, (b) how anemones open and close themselves, and (c) how anemones reproduce.

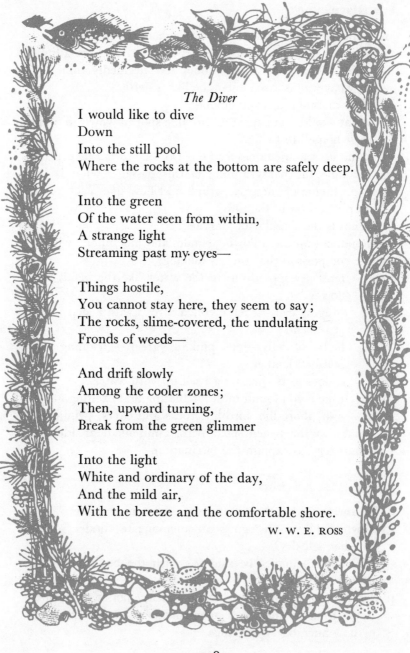

The Diver

I would like to dive
Down
Into the still pool
Where the rocks at the bottom are safely deep.

Into the green
Of the water seen from within,
A strange light
Streaming past my· eyes—

Things hostile,
You cannot stay here, they seem to say;
The rocks, slime-covered, the undulating
Fronds of weeds—

And drift slowly
Among the cooler zones;
Then, upward turning,
Break from the green glimmer

Into the light
White and ordinary of the day,
And the mild air,
With the breeze and the comfortable shore.

W. W. E. ROSS

Discussing The Poem

1. What are the contrasts between the underwater world and the ordinary world?
2. What is meant by the following?

    the undulating fronds   the cooler zones
    safely deep   the comfortable shore.

3. Why does the poet find the underwater world (a) hostile, (b) fascinating?

Method Exercises

Because this passage is from a factual book, it is written in a rather impersonal style. An important element of this is the use of the PASSIVE VOICE: instead of "Many people have known anemones to seize quite large animals," the writer has put:

    Anemones have been known to seize quite large animals.

And instead of "thousands of stinging cells stud these waving tentacles", she writes:

    These waving tentacles are studded with thousands of stinging cells.

The first version in each of these cases is called ACTIVE: the subjects ("many people" and "stinging cells") are *doing* something actively. Why is *passive* a good term for the second versions? What are the subjects of the verbs "have been known" and "are studded"?

Exercise 1. Give the active version of these other examples from the passage: the passive verbs are already in italics:

(a) Many people *are* still *puzzled* as to whether they are plants or animals.
(b) Shrimps, crabs, worms and small fish *are* first *paralysed* and then *consumed*.
(c) Large animals *are drawn in* slowly, by degrees.
(d) Later the undigested parts *are ejected* out of its mouth.
(e) The moment contact *is made*, the tentacles begin to close.
(f) If the pools *are left* high and dry, the anemones close.
(g) Their tentacles *are withdrawn* and *tucked away*.

Exercise 2. When we turn active voice to passive voice we take the natural object of the verb and make it subject. Only transitive verbs, therefore, can be passive. Take the objects of the verbs in the following active sentences, and make them the subjects, turning the verbs into the passive voice. Notice in these examples that we can retain the original subject by putting it after the word "by"—but often there is no point in doing so.

Active: People *find* anemones in rock pools.
Passive: Anemones *are found* in rock pools.
Active: My grandfather *was designing* that bridge in 1922.
Passive: That bridge *was being designed* by my grandfather in 1922.
    Be careful to keep the tenses the same, in the passive.
(a) Aunt Jane rode this bicycle.
(b) A scorer keeps the score in cricket.
(c) The voters elected him to Parliament.
(d) They sell vinegar here by the litre.
(e) A special deputation will meet the Queen.
(f) Someone will launch the new liner on Friday.
(g) A primitive man probably invented the wheel by accident.
(h) A bullet or something has wounded the general in the arm.
(i) A shower of tomatoes, bad eggs, cabbages and other rubbish met the official as he spoke.
(j) They are postponing the match until next week.

Exercise 3. In Chapter Eleven we noted that commas are used to mark off phrases (or clauses) "aside" from the main sentence, *in parenthesis* or *in apposition*. (Look these terms up if you have forgotten them.) In the passage in this chapter the writer has used commas once in this way:
    Later the undigested parts, shell, horny legs, etc., are ejected out of its mouth.
She has also used a pair of dashes in another sentence for this same purpose. Find these.

The following sentences contain examples of these, and the other uses of commas, as well as titles and special names that require inverted commas and some capital letters. In one case, there are *two* sentences in one question. Rewrite them all with the necessary punctuation:

(a) sea anemones called flower animals by the greeks are in fact animals

(b) many interesting creatures live along the sea shore on the sands in the pools under the rocks and in caves

(c) along the edge of the sea contains information about sea-nettles sponges shell-fish of all kinds sand-borers crabs mussels shrimps worms and all kinds of sea-creatures

(d) jill norman who wrote the book did the illustrations shells plants and sea-creatures herself

(e) the octopus with its large eyes horny beak and eight arms feeds on crabs lobsters etc catching its prey by grasping it in its powerful arms

(f) octopuses shy but intelligent creatures will often make collections of crabs before eating them they will also stand guard over mussels or clams for hours knowing that eventually they must open their shells to feed when the octopus will quickly slip a stone in the opening so that his arms can easily extract the soft interior

Exercise 4. Here are some word games.

(a) Take the letters BAN and see if you can remember (or, if necessary, look up in a dictionary) words beginning with BAN–that fit the following clues:

     e.g. This BAN is a tropical fruit—BANANA.

  i. This BAN is commonplace.

  ii. This BAN is a musical instrument.

  iii. This BAN is a richly coloured spotted handkerchief.

iv. This BAN is an outlaw.
v. This BAN is bow-legged.
vi. This BAN is a poison
vii. This BAN is without money.
viii. This BAN is a Scottish loaf.
ix. This BAN is a spirit of doom.
x. This BAN is a small kind of hen.

Make up other series of your own based on MAN, CAT, PAL or others of your own choice—you will need a dictionary for finding words and making up suitable clues.

(b) See how many words you can make out of the letters in a given word. For instance, the letters in NAMELESS will make (at least): name, less, seal, am, ma, man, mane, mean, meal, lease, maneless, mess, measles, lame, lameness, same, seem, seam, seen, sane, male, mass, slam, lessen, lane, lass, lea, la, me, sale, see, sea, ass, alms, ale, an, a.
(But "sameness" should *not* be in the list, because it would need *three* s's.)
See how many words you can make out of the letters in each of the following:

| homeward | passage | deliver |
| parole | testify | ourselves |

Find other words that can similarly be made into many more.

(c) Here is a *word chain* in which FOOL is changed into WISE in six moves, each move being the alteration of *one* letter only, to make another acceptable word (that you would find in a dictionary).

F O O L
F O O D
F O N D
F I N D
F I N E
W I N E
W I S E

Change the following in the shortest possible number of moves:

BOAT to CASH   FALL to RISE
SHIP to ROCK   HEAD to TAIL

Make up others of your own.

(d) These are known as *word squares:*

I	N	T	O
N	E	E	D
T	E	N	D
O	D	D	S

S	T	R	A	P
T	R	A	S	H
R	A	D	I	O
A	S	I	A	N
P	H	O	N	E

E	L	S	E
L	E	E	R
S	E	A	R
E	R	R	S

Notice how the words are complete and make sense both across and down. How does it differ from the normal crossword? Try to make up a fourth word square from the following clues to the words that make it up:

1. Always replies when you call.
2. Underneath your mouth.
3. An indication or suggestion.
4. To a position on.

Now see if you can devise some word squares (with clues) of your own.

Writing Your Own

What features of Jill Norman's style make it appropriate to conveying information? Notice how she makes the passage interesting by packing a great many fascinating details into the passage, and dealing logically with the material step by step, but she does not talk about herself or her own experiences directly: to do so would reduce the amount of information. Yet clearly she *does* know what she is writing about from first-hand experience; this allows her to describe vividly with interesting comparisons.

243

Such writing is often called EXPOSITION: clear, interesting description that is neither personal nor imaginative. Attempt your own piece of exposition on some subject you know something about, or after you have looked up the facts and made full notes on them. Notes will in any case help you to get the facts into an interesting and logical order. Notice also how Jill Norman *began* her account.

Choose a subject you can find information on; here are some suggestions:

Some species of fish, bird, mammal or insect—how they hunt, live and reproduce.

Some outstanding invention or discovery, its author(s) and its importance.

Your own hobby, the pleasure it gives and the equipment and practice required.

Your favourite writer, his books and his own life.

How to do something or make something.

The development of something, such as hovercraft, or space-craft.

Things To Do

1. If you are looking forward to any visits to the seaside, or a holiday by the sea, prepare illustrated lists of the shells, the fish, the shore creatures, the birds and the plants you may expect to see, catch or collect.

Use appropriate books from the library, making a sketch and writing a few lines for each item. Look in section 574.92, and through the sections 590 to 598.2.

2. Prepare a one-minute talk advocating one particular kind of holiday, such as camping, mountain climbing, caravanning, touring, a farm holiday, a sailing holiday, etc. Give reasons why you think this enjoyable and worth-while.

3. Write a poem, a description, or a fantastic story about the world under the sea, weird, silent, mysterious and beautiful.

4. Find out all you can about methods of diving, exploring, travelling and living under water. Investigate submarines and diving bells and the aqualung. Find out about pearl-fishers and those who do underwater archaeology or prospecting. Describe the apparatus an amateur needs to start diving in a modest way in rivers, lakes or at the seaside. Sea-diving is classified in the library as 626–627 and diving as a sport at 797.23; submarine craft will be at 623.8.

Books To Read

Along the Edge of the Sea by JILL NORMAN (Hutchinson)
This is a particularly interesting and well-illustrated book, explaining in simple terms about the often brilliant and exotic creatures that live under stones, in caves, in pools and among the seaweed along the shores of Britain. (Classified as 592).
The Summer People by JOHN ROWE TOWNSEND (O.U.P.)
A seaside holiday in the summer of 1939 is the setting for this family story of teenage love and jealousy, set against the looming threat of war, and in a cottage perilously close to the edge of a crumbling cliff-face.
The Racketty Street Gang by LEONARD H. EVERS (Brockhampton)
This gang of boys live in a street on Sydney Harbour and spend their spare time playing football and experimenting with skin-diving. They are intrigued by the unpleasant Tommo's activities in the mysterious boat-yard; and Anton's father is worried about an episode during the war, and constantly on the watch for trouble.
Jersey Adventure by VIOLA BAYLEY (Dent)
Viola Bayley's adventure stories are exciting tales of mystery. In this one, the young people are students doing summer holiday work on Jersey, but they find themselves inevitably drawn into deception and danger among the islands.

Supplementary Exercises

Analysis Exercise 5

Since a *complement* is different from an object, it appears in a different position in graphic analysis:

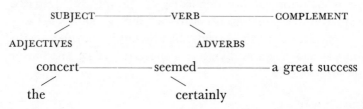

Notice that, although the subject is analysed into subject word and accompanying adjective(s), the complement is left *complete*.

(a) Analyse the following; each has a noun complement.

   i. My best friend was a boy from New Zealand.

  ii. The burglar returned a reformed character.

 iii. That train would have been a wreck.

 iv. We might be the only survivors.

   v. George Tomkins will be best man at the wedding.

 vi. The plan appeared a good one.

vii. Has her father become town clerk yet?

viii. Mr. Ponsonby remained caretaker of the school.

 ix. Be a man!

   x. Surely they are our best hockey players.

(b) Some of the following sentences have adjective complements; two do not have complements at all. Analyse them all:

   i. I was sick.

  ii. They were very tired after the journey.

 iii. They seemed very pleased with themselves.

 iv. Will you be happy?

   v. Will you be there?

 vi. The shop round the corner was very clean.

vii. The shop round the corner was selling tomatoes.

viii. This is London, capital of England.

 ix. Is the tomato soup ready?

   x. What is the answer?

Analysis Exercise 6

In Chapter 14 we saw that some verbs can take two distinct objects of different kinds. In graphic analysis the *indirect object* is indicated by a wavy line down to the right, thus:

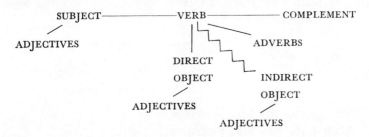

Notice that adjectives can again be split off from the indirect object word, as in this example:

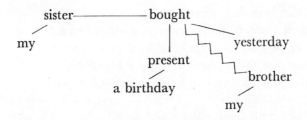

What statement sentence has been analysed here?

Analyse the following sentences; each one contains an indirect object.

(a) We can make them a patchwork quilt.
(b) The booking office found them accommodation.
(c) A man with ten pence once lent his companion five.
(d) I want to tell you something.
(e) Did she send her mother a card?
(f) What did you ask me?
(g) The repair cost him all his savings.
(h) Will you give me a ride?
(i) Now the audience can ask the speaker any questions about his talk.
(j) Draw me a picture of it.

247

Analysis Exercise 7

Passive verbs (see Chapter 18) can be analysed exactly like active ones: it is simply necessary to think carefully about what is the subject of the verb. Notice that any phrase introduced by the word "by", and attached to the passive verb, is an *adverb phrase*. For example:

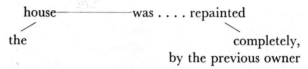

house————————was . . . . repainted

the

completely,

by the previous owner

What sentence has been analysed here?

Analyse the following sentences:

(a) The parcel had been completely lost.
(b) She was promised a pony last year.
(c) Her parents promised it her.
(d) I had been invited to a party.
(e) Most Roman roads were made quite straight.
(f) The new factory was built by a new process.
(g) The new factory was built by a new firm.
(h) The new factory was built by the end of July.
(i) The aircraft company built a new factory for themselves.
(j) They built themselves a new factory.

Analysis Exercise 8

In analysing the following, which represent all the various types of simple sentences, remember that any question words will be either pronouns (subject or object) or adjectives (attached to subject or object) or adverbs (attached to the verb). What question has been analysed in this example?

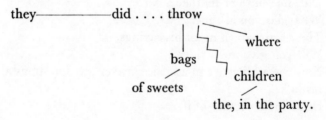

they————————did . . . . throw

bags

of sweets

where

children

the, in the party.

Analyse the following:
- (a) Where are you going?
- (b) I am going to the club tonight.
- (c) They offered me a cheap, second-hand cycle.
- (d) It was rather rusty.
- (e) It was basically a good machine.
- (f) The man in the end house seems rather eccentric.
- (g) He puts all his washing out in the middle of the night.
- (h) Why is that so odd?
- (i) It will all dry during the day.
- (j) Perhaps he works on shift work.
- (k) He works in the factory down the road.
- (l) What did the Headmaster give you just now?
- (m) Whom did he want?
- (n) Johnny was caught up on the roof.
- (o) How did he climb up there?

Revision Exercise 7

Here are some common prefixes and suffixes:

prefixes: pre-, mis-, re-, dis-, un-;

suffixes: -able, -ible, -ion, -y, -ment, -ful.

By taking a simple short word and adding one or more of these additional syllables, see how many more words you can make:

e.g., *sent:* present, presentable, unpresentable, presentably, presentiment, dissent, represent, representation, misrepresent, misrepresentation, resent, resentful, resentfully, etc.

Using only suffixes and prefixes from the above list, make as many new words as possible from the following. In each case make sure that you spell them correctly and that you know what they mean:

manage	form	organize
charge	pronounce	engage

(a) In each of the following you are given several *synonyms* and four or five sentences, each with a blank. Choose the synonyms that will best fit into these particular sentences; the first sentence has been completed for you. Rewrite the others.

i. assigned, awarded, bestowed, conferred, gave, granted.

     e.g., They <u>assigned</u> me a place to park.

     She——her friend a birthday present.

     The Queen has——a title on the Prime Minister.

     The magistrate——his petition.

     They——the first prize to the new variety of rose.

ii. felt, fingered, groped, handled, touched.

     As soon as I——the hedgehog, it curled up.

     I——the stove to see if it was still at all warm.

     When you have——as many problem cases as she has, you will understand.

     In the darkness we——for the door-handle.

iii. bid, offer, overture, proposition, tender.

     We put a——to him, that he could have all the goods at half-price, or not at all.

     If it is auctioned, the necklace will go to the highest——.

     His firm put in a——for the contract, but their rivals were asking less.

     We have made you a firm——for the property and you can take it or leave it.

iv. active, brisk, frisky, spry, vivacious.

     The committee has the matter under——consideration.

     The——laughter rapidly dispelled the gloom.

     The leader was——and energetic.

     The lambs were——.

v. gradually, languidly, slackly, sluggishly, stagnantly.

     He held the rope——, not expecting any strain on it.

     In the dry season, the river flows——by the castle.

     They were——reaching their goal.

     She answered——and without interest.

(b) Try to compose sentences of your own to illustrate subtle differences in meaning between these groups of synonyms:
i. annex, earn, glean, procure, win, (*verbs*).
ii. fodder, food, nourishment, provender, rations, (*nouns*).
(c) Find one or more *antonyms* for each group of synonyms in (a) and (b).

Revision Exercise 9

Each of the following sentences contains *two mistakes* of grammar, spelling or style (*not* punctuation). After studying Books One and Two you should be able to correct these and explain why the versions printed here are wrong.

e.g., No one in that vast crowd in the square have the least idea what they're there for.

Answer: No one in that vast crowd in the square *has* the least idea what *he's* there for.

("No one" is singular—it must therefore be subject of the singular verb "has" and be represented by the singular pronoun "he"—again with the singular verb "is".)

(a) Yours was worser than the best of those two.
(b) I done all me homework and went off for the weekend.
(c) They would of wanted to do everything theirselves.
(d) They was quite certain they been robbed of all their money while they slept.
(e) You lied when you said you layed an egg where you lied.
(f) They was forced to evacuate the camp by a leaking main sewer.
(g) The fog creeping over the landscape, reducing visibility too nil.
(h) Who's book was that one laying on the table?
(i) Whom do you think I am? They're keeper?
(j) Looking down from the spire, there view of the whole town was magnificent.

251

Rewrite the following description inserting all the remaining punctuation and capital letters. It is all one paragraph.

there were ruddy brown-faced broad-girthed Spanish Onions shining in the fatness of their growth like spanish friars; and winking from their shelves in wanton slyness at the girls as they went by, and glanced demurely at the hung-up mistletoe there were pears and apples clustered high in blooming pyramids; there were bunches of grapes made in the shopkeepers benevolence to dangle from conspicuous hooks that peoples mouths might water gratis as they passed; there were piles of filberts mossy and brown recalling in their fragrance ancient walks among the woods and pleasant shufflings ankle deep through withered leaves; there were norfolk biffins squab and swarthy setting off the yellow of the oranges and lemons and in the great compactness of their juicy persons urgently entreating and beseeching to be carried home in paper bags and eaten after dinner the very gold and silver fish set forth among these choice fruits in a bowl though members of a dull and stagnant-blooded race appeared to know that there was something going on; and to a fish went gasping round and round their little world in slow and passionless excitement.

(from *A Christmas Carol*)

(a) Write down the positive, comparative and superlative forms of each of these adjectives.

e.g. good: good—better—best.

In at least one case no comparative or superlative is possible—discuss why.

lovely	ugly	much	perfect	bad
hopeful	alone	many	poor	intolerable
sure	lively	feeble	comfortable	faithful

(b) Rearrange the following groups of words (now in alphabetical order) in order of "intensity"; thus

> moon, planet, star, galaxy, universe,

is a series that moves from smaller to larger.
- i. adequate, excellent, exceptional, fair, good.
- ii. careful, frugal, grudging, mean, miserly.
- iii. amble, race, run, streak, trot.
- iv. dawdle, linger, plod, stroll, tarry.
- v. captain, corporal, lance-corporal, second lieutenant, sergeant-major.

Revision Exercise 12

If you have studied Book Two thoroughly, you should be able to rewrite the following statements inserting the correct word or words to complete each one. If you cannot do this, refer back to the appropriate chapter.

(a) Words of similar meaning are called . . . . and those of opposite meaning are called . . . .

(b) A direct comparison between two things in one or more particular respects is called a . . . .

(c) A *metaphor* is a . . . . comparison, in which one thing is treated as if . . . .

(d) A . . . . is a group of words (without a verb) which, as a group, does the work of an adverb, adjective or noun in a sentence.

(e) The verb "to be" and other "being verbs" often take . . . . instead of objects.

(f) When verbs have two distinct objects, the person or thing for whom or to whom the action happens is called the . . . . object.

(g) The repetition of similar consonant sounds is called . . ., and . . . . is the use of words to suggest or represent actual sounds (e.g., "splash").

(h) The part or form of a verb ending in -ing is called a . . . . and this is frequently used as an adjective.

(i) Verbs that require objects to complete their sense are called . . . . verbs.

Books Recommended

An alphabetical author index of the books recommended in the Books To Read sections in this volume.

254

MONTGOMERY, RUTHERFORD	*Carcajou*	...	Longmans
NAUGHTON, BILL	*The Goalkeeper's Revenge* ...	...	Heinemann; Penguin; (Macmillan without "other stories")
NORMAN, JILL	*Along the Edge of the Sea* ...	...	Hutchinson
O'BRIAN, PATRICK	*The Golden Ocean*... ...	...	Macmillan; Penguin
O'HARA, MARY	*My Friend Flicka*	...	Methuen; Mayflower
PEARCE, A. PHILIPPA	*Tom's Midnight Garden* ...	...	O.U.P.; Penguin
	A Dog So Small	...	Longman; Penguin
PRODANOVIC, NADA CURCIJA	*Ballerina*	...	O.U.P.
RANSOME, ARTHUR	*We Didn't Mean to Go to Sea* and *Winter Holiday*... ...	...	Cape; Penguin
RAWLINGS, MARJORIE KINNAN	*The Yearling*	...	Heinemann
SCOTT, CAPT. R. F.	*Scott's Last Expedition* ...	...	Murray; Tandem
SERRAILLIER, IAN	*The Gorgon's Head*, *The Way of Danger*		Heinemann; O.U.P.
	The Ivory Horn		Heinemann
	The Silver Sword		Cape; Heinemann; Penguin
SEVERN, DAVID	*The Future Took Us* ...	...	Penguin
SNYDER, ZILPHA KEATLEY	*The Changeling* ...	...	Lutterworth
SOUTHALL, IVAN	*Hills End*	...	Angus; Penguin
STAGG, JAMES	*Clarion Call*	...	Dent
STORR, CATHERINE	*Marianne Dreams*... ...	...	Penguin
STREATFEILD, NOEL	*White Boots*	...	Collins; Penguin
SWIFT, JONATHAN	*Gulliver's Travels*	...	Various
THOMPSON, DIANA PULLEIN	*The Secret Dog*	...	Collins
TOWNSEND, JOHN ROWE	*The Summer People* ...	...	O.U.P.
TREASE, GEOFFREY	*The Maythorn Story* ...	...	Heinemann
UTTLEY, ALISON	*A Traveller in Time* ...	...	Faber and Faber
VAN DER LOEFF, ANNA RUTGER	*Avalanche*...	...	Brockhampton; Penguin
VIPONT, ELFRIDA	*The Lark in the Morn* ...	...	O.U.P.
WALSH, JILL PATON	*The Dolphin Crossing* ...	...	Macmillan; Penguin
WARNER, REX	*Greeks and Trojans* ...	...	Heinemann
WESTALL, ROBERT	*The Machine-Gunners* ...	...	Macmillan
WILDER, LAURA INGALLS	*The Long Winter* ...	...	Lutterworth; Penguin
WOOLLEY, SIR LEONARD	*Digging Up the Past* ...	...	Benn
YOUNG, STANLEY	*Mayflower Boy*	...	Pickering & Inglis
VARIOUS AUTHORS	*The Great Composers* (series)	...	Faber and Faber

Index

An alphabetical list of the method work (only) in this volume. The references are to page numbers.